Organizing Instruction in Early Childhood

A Handbook of Assessment and Activities

Sue Clark Wortham

THE UNIVERSITY OF TEXAS AT SAN ANTONIO

ALLYN AND BACON, INC.

Boston   London   Sydney   Toronto

Library of Congress Cataloging in Publication Data

Wortham, Sue Clark, 1935–
  Organizing instruction in early childhood.

  Includes bibliographies and index.
  1. Curriculum development. 2. Concept learning.
3. Motor learning. 4. Exceptional children—Education.
5. Play. I. Title.
LB1570.W68   1984   372.19   83–21537
ISBN 0–205–08144–4

Printed in the United States of America
10 9 8 7 6 5 4 3 2 1   88 87 86 85 84

Organizing Instruction
in Early Childhood

Contents

Preface

This book was written in response to requests from students and teachers who asked for ways to manage children more effectively and to design a developmentally appropriate curriculum for their classrooms or early childhood centers.

While there are abundant curriculum resources available for use with young children, educators in various types of early childhood settings are interested in developing their own curriculum. This handbook meets that need by demonstrating how a curriculum can be designed from a skills continuum. Examples of practical activities are included to encourage teachers to feel confident that teacher-designed activities can be easily constructed for a curriculum using found materials.

The handbook is organized to accommodate various types of instructional organization and teaching styles. Each component of an early childhood curriculum, represented by a section of the Frost Wortham Developmental Checklist is explained in a chapter. Relevant activities which are correlated with the checklist are also a part of each chapter. Adaptation of a developmental curriculum for special populations is also addressed.

Teachers do not learn how to improve their teaching by themselves, nor are new teaching ideas generated and developed from theory alone. The strategies in this book were originally conceptualized and developed by a group of dedicated teachers who comprised the staff of Bonham Elementary School, a kindergarten school in San Marcos, Texas, in the 1970s. Special thanks go to Yolanda Almendariz, Gloria Flores, and Carolyn Jackson, who as fellow teachers and team leaders struggled to develop an early childhood model, and also to LaRue Miller, a principal who encouraged and facilitated innovative teaching.

A major and ongoing influence in my own growth as a professional early childhood educator is Joe Frost at the University of Texas at Austin. As with all his graduate and former graduate students, Joe offers leadership, encouragement, and opportunities to become competent. I thank him for helping me to develop the confidence to evolve my own ideas for early childhood education and for including me in his professional opportunities for consulting, early childhood model and curriculum development, and teacher training. Because Joe believes in my potential to make a contribution to the field, I am able to extend my understanding and skills as an educator.

My own students have made the book possible. Under my supervision, undergraduate students at the University of Texas at San Antonio developed the ideas and materials for curriculum activities. They include Marilyn Barry, Ronnie Beaty, Leisa Bonewald, Lucy Braun, Lourdes Elizondo, Carolyn Elledge, Zaneta Flores, Lucy French, Ginny Fuller, Carmen Gamez, Mary Jane Garza, Sylvia Holub, Yolanda Jackson, Ruth Jung, Mary Ann Keyland, Joanne Lyons, Barbara McMahon, Garizela Pena, Karla Salzman, Cynthia Sawyer, June Sebesta, Laura Sherman, Brenda Spire, Cheryl Stuckey, and Yolanda Yzaguirre. Graduate students who participated in validating checklists are Mary Barrera, Shirley Berchelman, Laquita Boyd, Cynthia Chavez, Ana Diaz, Juanita Fox, Susan Frawley, Carol Ann Gomez, Angie Hoyt, Joan Lanius, Jolene Lopez, Evangie Maldonado, Linda Kay Montgomery, Charlotte Mulkey, Kim Nelson, Christine Rhodes, Dora Ruvalcaba, Rachel Sanchez, Sandra Jo Sanchez, Johnnie Stoeltje, and Patsy Wood.

Many early childhood centers in the San Antonio area graciously permitted students to work with their children using activities to validate the checklists of skills. I thank the following centers for their cooperation: Santa Rosa Hospital Child Care Center, Orange Goose Schools 1 and 7, Wesleyan Child Care Center, La Petite Academy, Bethel United Methodist Child Care Center, Los Angeles Heights United Methodist Day Care Center and Kindergarten, Our Savior's Advent Lutheran Church Day Care Center, and St. Mary's University Child Care Center. Crockett Elementary School in San Marcos, Texas, provided children for additional validation of some checklist objectives.

Students in "Guidance of Young Children in Groups" (ECE 4103), a course I teach at the University of Texas at San Antonio, over a period of semesters provided valuable feedback on book content as the first drafts were developed. Marilyn Mott, a fellow instructor for the course, also contributed information on content effectiveness as a textbook.

My sister, Mary Polk, and Pat Trusten helped me with the typing.

It is very convenient to live within a family of artists. I thank my husband, Marshal, for many hours of translating activities into a visual form.

Finally, I need to express my appreciation to my son, Ben, who as a teenager cooks gourmet meals and repairs cars, appliances, typewriters, and any other mysterious equipment in his efforts to keep his parents organized and functioning.

Organizing Instruction
in Early Childhood

CHAPTER **1**

An Introduction

Teachers in early childhood classrooms today face complex problems in meeting the learning needs of the children they teach. Bombarded with new information about learning, an abundance of commercial materials, and escalating expectations from the home, community, and governmental agencies, teachers are looking for answers that will result in maximum improvement of instruction but that are also manageable.

Since the resurgence of interest in early childhood programs and the initiation of the Head Start movement in the 1960s, designers and publishers of curriculum resources are producing materials and kits that are represented as providing for all of the curriculum needs in the classroom. In many instances curriculum resources are selected by supervisory personnel rather than teachers, or they are inherited from previous instructors. Often, those who purchase curriculum kits are unaware of learning theories or of research conducted prior to publication and distribution of materials. School district administrators frequently make bulk purchases of materials without evaluating whether the materials are appropriate for the population of young children served by the schools in their district. As teachers try to use the available curriculum resources, they may discover a mismatch between the activities they are providing and the children participating in the activities. Teachers also frequently discover that they lack sufficient resources to adequately provide a broad range of experiences for the children. At the other extreme are the teachers who have more curriculum materials than they can properly analyze or use; eventually they leave most of the materials unopened or use them without first determining the purpose intended by the developers.

For many generations preschool classrooms reflected a maturationist theory of child development. School activities used with children under six were designed to provide social and cognitive experiences that would prepare students to enter primary school. Most of the instruction provided by teachers was planned for the entire class. As the result of various factors—including the work of Jean Piaget, Benjamin Bloom, and Jerome Bruner and information gained from the Head Start movement—early childhood programs are seen as a vital period for learning rather than as a period of preparation. As more data are reported on how children develop and learn, as well as the importance of early experiences, teachers are seeking information about appropriate strategies to use in the school environment. Guidelines established by state and federal agencies reflect the importance of understanding individual differences in children's development. These agencies expect preschool and elementary classrooms to adjust instruction to the individual language, cognitive, and affective needs of the students.

Teachers sometimes discover that providing appropriate learning experiences for individual children within a group setting can be a bewildering task. Initially the question is how to determine what the scope of instruction will be for the year, followed by the problem of how to determine what the children already know and are ready to learn next. Finally, managing the classroom that will provide for differences in learning needs can become a source of anxiety for the teacher who lacks experience in organizing the environment for children who are functioning at several developmental levels.

Teachers also want to know how to design a curriculum that includes a comprehensive program for all areas of growth for the young child. While the "back to basics" movement has increased the pressures to stress math and reading-readiness activities, children still need a balanced experience that provides for exploration in the fine arts and the natural and social sciences, as well as for physical activities necessary for the total development of the young child. Preservice training for early childhood educators includes initial exposure to the importance of the various components of an early childhood program; nevertheless, practicing teachers often find it difficult to maintain a proper perspective when faced with pressures to accelerate children's preparation for the basics. In these circumstances it seems impossible to fulfill all the expectations and external pressures and still provide sound, developmentally appropriate experiences that allow for student-centered and student-initiated learning.

The pervasive dichotomy between instruction in the primary grades and preschool classrooms also presents problems for teachers. Traditionally, elementary school teachers and preschool teachers have been prepared differently for teaching. While preschool educators have had instruction in child development and its implications for classroom experiences, elementary teachers have received training that stresses methodology for teaching the various subjects. Although students in universities today are receiving more similar training whether they plan to teach children under six or in the primary grades, instruction still varies widely for the two levels. Primary school teachers are concerned about their students who are "immature" and who do not benefit from classroom instruction. Kindergarten teachers are equally frustrated by students who are bored with most preschool activities and who show signs of being able to read. Teachers at both levels express a need to understand better how the young child learns and how they can adapt to their classrooms teaching strategies that will provide more continuity between preschool and primary grades.

Although the checklist in this handbook provides a model for developing curriculum, the content of the book can be used with some adaptation to other locally or commercially developed checklists of objectives. Teachers who teach with kits and other instructional approaches can use the suggestions and ideas to enhance their resources for child-centered activities without implementing the structure of a checklist. Nevertheless, the strategies presented in this text will allow the teacher to initiate individualized instruction with a system easy to understand and use.

This volume addresses many of the issues just discussed. As a result of working with students at the preservice level and guiding teachers who are encountering these and similar problems, the Frost Wortham Developmental Checklist was developed and refined through its use in classrooms with various ethnic and socioeconomic populations, including bilingual children and children with learning handicaps. In the following chapters the checklist is used as a framework for planning and implementing a curriculum that provides for individual needs and accounts for a sound early childhood curriculum without abandoning the child-initiated discovery approach to learning so necessary for the optimal growth and development of young children.

CHAPTER **2**

Developmental Levels
of Children

HOW CHILDREN LEARN IN EARLY CHILDHOOD

Within the last three decades, the new information that has become available on how infants and children develop and learn has had a tremendous impact on instructional programs for young children. One source is Head Start, a federally funded program for preschool children from low income homes that provides academic, social, and health services to prepare children better for successful learning when they enter public school. Follow Through, an extension of Head Start, seeks to extend the gains children made in Head Start into the elementary grades. As a result of the Head Start and Follow Through movements, which have implemented several theories of learning, we educators are trying to sort out methods, materials, and strategies to determine the most effective ways to teach the young child.

Fortunately we are in a period of renewed interest in early childhood and early childhood education. Educators have the opportunity to reflect on recent research, as well as on the more traditional practices, in order to help us make the match between how children learn and the learning experiences that should be provided in day care, public schools, and other early childhood programs. Investigators have been studying the significance of relationships between aspects of development of infants and young children and implications they have for the education of young children. In a society of changing social and economic practices, fewer children are cared for in the home during the preschool years. Developmental researchers are examining

4

the effect of day care on child development and on the quality of parent-child relationships. The influx of children into the United States who speak a variety of languages other than English has resulted in renewed efforts to provide instructional strategies that will ease adjustment of these children to educational settings where the language of education is English. Likewise, the policy of mainstreaming handicapped children into classrooms with normal children has necessitated the development of more sophisticated assessment tools and instructional planning. The study of these issues and others provides pieces of information that influence the nature of school environments and how learning experiences for children should be designed and implemented.

Our understanding of how children learn has a long history. It began in the eighteenth century with the initial belief of Johann Heinrich Pestalozzi and Jean Jacques Rousseau that childhood is a unique period in life and that children experience life differently from adults. Early childhood educators have since sought to determine that process in little children that allows them to learn. Although the advent of educational programs for young children occurred in the middle of the nineteenth century with the establishment of Froebel's kindergarten in Germany, early childhood programs today reflect contributions made by outstanding educators from Froebel's time to the present. Froebel believed that children should learn in an environment that was designed especially for them. In his kindergarten (literally, "child's garden") he provided play tools, or "gifts," for children to use to learn the properties of matter. His "occupations" were activities to be used with each gift (Ransbury, 1982).

In the early decades of the twentieth century, psychologists associated with the new field of psychology initiated the study of child development. G. Stanley Hall (1906) adhered to the recapitulation theory, which was based on the understanding that the child's development paralleled the evolutionary history of man. Although Hall's theory was later disregarded, he saw childhood as the recapitulation of the stages of development of man from a primitive to a civilized society.

Sigmund Freud formed a psychoanalytic view of development, which postulates the child progressing through stages of psychosexual behavior and development. On the basis of his work with adults, Freud (1938) determined that human behavior is motivated by the emotions. He felt that the human being has strong instinctive drives and unconscious memories, which may be significant determinants of behavior. Erik Erikson (1950), building on Freud's work, developed stages of growth in terms of interpersonal relationships in a social setting.

Arnold Gesell's maturationist theory was responsible for many educational practices established in the 1930s that still affect practices in educational programs today. Gesell (1954) described the growth and development of young children as progressing through experience and genetic inheritance. He proposed that all children mature through the same stages. Education and instruction are based on the maturation and readiness of the child. Much of the curriculum designed for a particular age or grade level in school follows the characteristics of a child at that age as described by Gesell.

In the 1950s and 1960s newer information about child development and learning has resulted in more emphasis on early experiences. From Benjamin Bloom we have learned that early experiences have an important effect on individual potential for learning. In his *Stability and Change in Human Characteristics* (1964), Bloom reported on the results of his longitudinal study of individual development that the early years are critical for the child's ability to learn. There is no other time in human life when so much is learned in so brief a period. Jerome Bruner has also stressed the learning potential of the early years by giving educators insight into how the organization of instruction can make it possible for young children to learn information that previously was introduced only to older children. In *The Process of Education* (1960), Bruner proposed that teachers should present information in a style that is compatible with the child's way of viewing things. Through more appropriate instructional planning the school environment could serve to increase the intellectual functioning of children. These and other authors have focused our attention on the tremendous potential that young children have for learning.

We have also gained new perspectives on how young children learn from the opposing views of B. F. Skinner and Jean Piaget. While Skinner (1953) saw learning as a response of the child to an external stimulus, Piaget (1952) described learning as being initiated by the child as he or she interacts with the environment. Skinner explained learning in terms of operant conditioning. If a desired behavior is reinforced or rewarded, it is more likely to recur, and if an inappropriate behavior is ignored, it is less likely to recur. Through the use of positive or negative responses to a child's behavior, the behavior can be conditioned.

Operant conditioning also explains how the child learns. When the child uses the correct answer or behavior in a learning activity, the response is rewarded. Incorrect answers are not rewarded. Learning occurs as the child uses adult cues or other types of feedback to determine which responses are correct. In programmed instruction or computer assisted instruction, feedback is provided by written materials, games, or electronic equipment. When the student makes a correct response, he or she advances to a new level of difficulty. Incorrect responses result in more learning episodes at the same level of difficulty until the student demonstrates mastery through the desired responses.

In Skinner's learning theory, outside forces control learning. Piaget, in contrast, proposed that the child, rather than the adult, initiates learning. The child learns as a result of acting on his or her environment. The child then uses broadened understanding resulting from these actions to make hypotheses for additional learning. According to Hohmann, Banet, and Weikart (1979, p. 3) the theory implies "that *the teacher is a supporter of develop-*

ment, and as such his or her prime goal is to promote *active learning* on the part of the child."

Piaget's theory of learning (1952) is divided into two components, the stage-dependent and stage-independent. In the stage-dependent component the growth of intelligence from birth through adolescence evolves through a series of three periods and many subperiods. The first period, the sensorimotor period with its six substages, lasts from birth to approximately eighteen months. During this period the infant and toddler uses his or her senses and physical actions to learn about the world.

In the second stage, the concrete operations period lasting from about age two to approximately age eleven, the child develops through two subperiods, the preoperational subperiod and the concrete operations subperiod. The preoperational subperiod (about age two to age seven) is of interest because it generally parallels the years of early childhood. During this period children judge physical characteristics by appearances. They do not possess the concept of conservation, that the amount or a quantity of a material stays the same when the appearance is altered. Likewise, the preoperations child cannot think simultaneously about two physical dimensions. When two sticks of equal length are arranged in a nonparallel position, the child will focus on the position rather than on the length of the sticks and will think that one is longer than the other. The child in the preoperations period is egocentric and therefore unable to appreciate the viewpoint of others or understand causality. Finally, preoperational children cannot understand the relationship between a whole and its parts. They can only think about one characteristic at a time (Sharp, 1969).

During the concrete operations subperiod the child overcomes many of the thought processes of the preoperations subperiod and is able to conserve quantity and number. The child also understands the relationship between a whole and its parts and can classify objects by attributes.

The third and last stage, the formal operations period, which lasts from ages eleven to fifteen, is characterized by abstract thinking. The adolescent is now approaching adult reasoning. Thought includes not only reality, but also potential reality or possibilities.

The stage-independent component of Piaget's theory is concerned with the process involved in the child's learning. According to Piaget, intelligence is dependent on adaptive behavior. When encountering new information the child adapts to the information using assimilation and accommodation. In assimilation the child integrates the new information with existing information. Accommodation involves adapting the existing information to include the new input. The mental structure or schema has changed or expanded to incorporate the new information.

Piaget, therefore, describes the development of the child as moving in stages from infancy, when the infant learns entirely through the senses and physical interaction, to later childhood, when the child functions at the level of formal operations, where the abstract symbol and written word can be used. In between these stages the child moves through intermediate periods in a progression from concrete to abstract learning. The stage-independent component is the process involved that alters the child's understanding of reality as he or she develops.

The crucial implication of Piaget's theory for early childhood educators is the child's style or mode of learning in the preoperational period. During this period the child is using real experiences with objects or events to internalize and process the learning of concepts.

There are other important points about Piaget's theory that teachers of young children need to remember. One is that the child does not leave one stage and enter another at a single point in time. The progress is gradual, with the child acquiring characteristics of a new stage at an uneven rate. Some characteristics are acquired before others.

More importantly, since the child develops at his or her own rate, new stages cannot be taught by adults. Children who are provided with stimulating experiences proceed through the stages more rapidly; however, children cannot be pushed into new stages as a result of instruction. The role of the teacher is to provide opportunities for children to explore, experiment, and construct with a variety of materials. The child's experiences with the environment are the powerful factors that promote learning and development.

In summary, what we have learned from the study of young children, especially in recent decades, has forced us to regard the young child as an involved learner, one who learns best by initiating and actively participating in learning experiences. In addition, each child develops and learns at an individual rate, with a personal learning style. The task of the teacher is to use this information to provide relevant learning experiences for all the children in the classroom.

HOW AN APPROPRIATE CURRICULUM IS DESIGNED FOR YOUNG CHILDREN

A stumbling block in designing an appropriate curriculum for young children in the past has been the different teaching practices used by kindergarten teachers on the one hand and primary school teachers on the other. While the preschool teacher has encouraged play and exploration of the learning environment, primary teachers frequently use workbooks and other paper-and-pencil activities for reinforcement of learning. Both levels of teaching, while very different, result in teachers encountering frustration with many of their students. Primary teachers are confronted each year with children who are too "immature" or who lack the readiness for work at the elementary level. Likewise, preschool teachers are puzzled by students who are bored or not responsive to the kindergarten curriculum.

An understanding of how young children learn in early childhood provides some clues to the problems these teachers encounter. The term *early childhood* can refer to the age span between three and eight years of age. Children within this age range are similar in how they learn. The child who is in nursery school, a day-care center, kindergarten, or primary school is at some stage of early childhood. Each child's development is different depending on the kinds of experiences that have been available in his or her world. Because children do not develop by chronological age alone, children at each age level are at various points on the developmental continuum. There is a wide disparity of development among children at each chronological level.

The teacher designing curriculum needs to be aware of developmental differences in the students in the classroom in order to design instructional activities that will challenge each student. As a result, instructional practices of primary and preschool classrooms should be more similar than different.

In the past, preschool environments were characterized by an informal or open environment. Children spent time each day in learning centers exploring with puzzles, manipulative materials, and other discovery activities. There were opportunities for formal group instruction, but large blocks of the day were typified by relaxed interaction between teachers and children as different activities took place. In the first grade the environment was more structured, with children spending long periods of the day being instructed formally by the teacher or occupied with written assignments to be completed at their desks. There was a sharp difference between the environmental settings and learning activities for preschool versus primary-age children.

Preschool classroom teachers have felt the pressure to provide more academic-readiness activities to "get children ready for first grade." As a result many preschool programs have become more structured. As teachers are expected to accelerate their students' preparation for academic instruction, children are spending longer periods of time completing workbook materials. Learning opportunities using concrete materials in centers receive less attention or have been relegated to "play periods," which are allowed after workbook assignments have been completed.

Educators should realize that there is a great need for continuity between preschool and the primary-level curriculum. Children in all early childhood years require an educational program that matches their level of development, regardless of chronological age. Teachers in preschool and early elementary programs have a responsibility to structure the curriculum so that their students can move through early childhood years with learning opportunities that are developmentally compatible with their ability to learn.

The student in early childhood needs to be an active, involved learner, with real experiences and many concrete materials available to explore and manipulate in the process of cognitive learning. If the teacher understands this, the classroom environment at all levels will become somewhat altered. Preschool environments, while retaining a child-centered, informal approach, will reflect the fact that, although children are chronologically the same age, developmentally they are different. More diversified activities will be provided to accommodate the different developmental levels. Thus for some children, more advanced learning activities previously delayed until first grade will be available within the setting that is arranged for active, child-directed learning. Primary-level classroom teachers, also recognizing the need of their children for active learning in later stages of early childhood, will expand their use of concrete learning materials and will include opportunities for children to determine how to use the materials. Primary-level teachers will also diversify learning experiences to accommodate the developmental levels of their students.

Through the Head Start movement in the 1960s, models developed providing valuable information on effective strategies that can be adopted by early childhood programs. Each model, as conceptualized by its developers, was unique in some respects; however, Spodek (1973) categorized most of the models as being behaviorist or phenomenological in origin. The behaviorist models follow the behavior-analysis theory of Skinner. Instructional goals are set for students, and teaching is considered to be the systematic management of the consequences of student behavior. Teacher attention and approval are used to reinforce desired student behaviors. Withholding attention or ignoring is used to extinguish inappropriate behaviors. Access to or denial of preferred activities is also used to achieve desired student behaviors (Bushell, 1982).

The phenomenological models are characterized by child-initiated learning based on Piaget's theory of development. Designed for children functioning in the preoperational period of development, phenomenological models allow children to learn through exploring and experimenting at their own level of development. The teacher facilitates learning by providing materials and activities that will foster the child's learning through active and direct experiences.

Some models were developed as combinations of theories or approaches to learning. Models using various theoretical approaches have been successful, depending on the type of evaluation used to assess them. Regardless of personal reactions to the opposing theories, all have contributed successful instructional and management strategies that can be used in early childhood classrooms.

One feature that all the models share is that each is based on a framework of goals and objectives. Regardless of the structure of the learning environment and the method used for children's learning, each model rests on some organization of experiences that are deemed appropriate for the early childhood student. Curriculum specialists have studied models' goals and objectives and have translated them into forms that fit varied types of early childhood settings. A commonly used form is the *skills continuum*, or *checklist*. The Frost Wortham Developmental Checklist is one example of a framework for curriculum that early childhood teachers can use to design and implement an instructional program.

UNDERSTANDING A DEVELOPMENTAL CHECKLIST

In recent years many efforts have been made to design curricula that will allow teachers to provide instructional experiences suitable for each child in the classroom. Recognizing that the range of learning achievement in any classroom can vary according to the child's level of development, educators have developed checklists of skills that will allow teachers to determine the level of instruction each child needs.

A skills continuum reflects both the scope of a curriculum and the sequence of skills to be learned in each curriculum area. The *scope of the curriculum* is the range of categories within a subject area. For instance, in the subject of reading the curriculum content can be divided into areas that include word-attack skills and comprehension. Each of these areas can be further subdivided to represent each type of skill within each area. Thus the category of word-attack skills can include phonic analysis, structural analysis, dictionary skills, and sight words. Likewise, the *sequence of skills* includes each category of the curriculum; however, the sequence refers to a hierarchical arrangement of skills from simple to complex or from easy to difficult. Skills checklists are often divided into levels or some type of arrangement to indicate divisions in the hierarchy of skills.

Skills continua are available from many sources. Newer editions of textbooks now include the scope and sequence of skills used in their programs. Producers of supplementary resources or systems for diagnosis and prescription also provide a scope and a sequence. Often school districts choose to design skills continua that will represent the unique nature of the curriculum content used in their schools.

Skills continua range from simple to complex and from brief to lengthy. If developers attempt to include every objective or skill taught at each level, the continuum usually is quite long. In contrast, if the continuum includes a representative sample of essential skills or objectives, the resulting checklist is more condensed.

A skills continuum or checklist can have many purposes for the classroom teacher. Of primary importance is its use as a framework for instruction. The skills continuum describes in a brief form the goals and objectives the teacher has for a content area. It provides accountability to the parents and the community by specifying what is being taught in the classroom.

As was stated previously, the skills continuum also provides a vehicle for individualizing instruction. As an alternative to whole-group instruction, the teacher can vary instruction for small groups or individuals depending on individual rates of learning and achievement.

Finally, the skills continuum frees the teacher from dependence on textbooks and on teacher guides for curriculum design. With the skills continuum available for delineating what to teach, the teacher has the opportunity to become the developer of the curriculum. Rather than being limited to following the suggestions of textbook developers, the teacher can use all available materials as resources to fit into plans for implementing the objectives outlined in the skills continuum.

THE FROST WORTHAM DEVELOPMENTAL CHECKLIST

The Frost Wortham Developmental Checklist was designed to provide a scope and sequence of skills and other indicators of development at the early childhood level of the school experience. (This checklist occurs in complete form at the end of the chapter, pp. 22–33, and is described in detail in the sections that follow.) The term *developmental* emphasizes that the checklist items are described in terms of development levels rather than age levels. The scope of the checklist includes all areas of the development of the young child, while the sequence attempts to include the range of development in the preschool years of early childhood.

The areas of development are described by the following classifications: Concept Development, Language Development, Social Play and Socializing, and Motor Development. These broad areas are used rather than more traditional descriptions such as art, social studies, and science because of the nature of learning and growth in the young child. The acquisition of concepts by the young child is more a question of how learning occurs than in what area of the curriculum the learning occurs. Because it is also difficult to separate learning objectives into content categories, it is more appropriate to describe objectives within broad arrangements. For example, the ability to name colors can be classified as belonging to math, science, or general concept development. Hopefully, the Frost Wortham Developmental Checklist minimizes this source of confusion.

Concept Development Checklists

Preschool children, particularly four and five year olds, are just becoming aware that mental processes exist independent of physical materials. Two- and three-year-old children are beginning to form concepts of thinking. (Wellman, 1982). Concept development refers to the organization of information as it is encountered by the child. In the checklists, concept development is further subdivided into the two categories of identification, discrimination, and classification skills and quantitative and problem-solving skills. *Identification* refers to identifying or naming within events or activities. *Discrimination* skills refers to activities in which the child can determine likenesses and differences in items or experiences. *Classification* is the ability to arrange objects or pictures of items into specified categories.

In the mathematics category of concept development, subcategories are quantitative and problem solving. *Quantitative* skills refer to acquisition of various objectives such as counting, one-to-one correspondence, and ordering or combining sets, while *problem solving* is related to developmental activities such as comparing volumes in different containers. It should be pointed out, however, that these subcategories overlap, because math concepts involve problem solving and vice versa.

Language Development Checklists

Language development refers to the process whereby children learn to speak and understand their native tongue. The language development checklist has been broadened to include both oral language development and reading readiness. *Language development* describes the development of syntax and language usage, while *reading readiness* includes the skills and other indicators leading to beginning reading. Vocabulary development obviously is not limited to this category, but is found in all parts of the checklist. Vocabulary is developed in all kinds of early childhood experiences.

Dramatic Play

Dramatic play can be defined as those experiences that extend the child's understanding of his or her place in the world. Role playing, puppetry, building, painting, and playing in various environments are all a part of dramatic play. Dramatic play is a subcategory within the Social Play and Socializing Checklist.

Social Play and Socializing Checklist

Social play and socializing skills trace the behaviors in school that enable the child to function as part of a group and to interact in appropriate ways with other children and adults. Social play also includes the development of play behaviors and the use of different types of play for learning.

Motor Development Checklists

Motor development checklists describe the development of gross and fine motor skills. *Gross motor skills* refers to large muscle development, movements of the entire body, or major parts of the body. *Fine motor skills* refers to small muscle development, or movements requiring dexterity or precision. The motor development checklists are also related to the coordination of the eye and hand and to self-help skills such as buttoning clothes and using a knife and fork to eat.

CHECKLIST ORGANIZATION

The checklists have a hierarchical arrangement or sequence. Each part of the checklist is divided into Levels III, IV, and V (with the exception of reading readiness, which covers only Level V). Although the progress of a child through the levels is not necessarily age related, the levels themselves are generally oriented to ages three through five. Individual children master the skills at each level according to their development, not their chronological age. Depending on previous experiences, maturation, and inherent ability, the child may have developed more in some areas than others. For example, the child's language development might be more advanced than his or her fine motor skills.

The sequential nature of the checklists also fits the development of diverse learners in the classroom. The gifted child may be challenged by beginning at the upper levels of the checklist and moving on to activities that previously were not introduced until the primary grades. Likewise, if the teacher finds one level too difficult for some children, activities from lower levels may be introduced to ensure success. Depending on the type of disability, handicapped children might be unable to function in some areas of the skills continuum but could become actively involve in other categories. Whatever the nature of each child, the teacher can use the checklist to provide the kind of experiences each child needs in order to learn and develop.

USING THE DEVELOPMENTAL CHECKLIST AS A FRAMEWORK FOR INSTRUCTION

During the 1960s and early 1970s many experimental programs were developed to improve instruction for various populations of children who did not achieve as well as middle-class children. These projects were federally funded within the Head Start movement and were designed from theories of learning that also had emerged in the 1950s and 1960s. As previously described, some projects developed from a single theorist, while others reflected a combination of theories. Spodek (1973) categorized the early childhood programs into two models of humans, behavioral and phenomenological, as described by Hitt (1969). The behavioral model of humans assumes that the behavior of the child is determined by external persons and events. The teacher provides the stimuli for learning, while the child is the recipient. The teacher uses a reward system to shape the child's responses so that the desired learning can occur. Behaviorist models are characterized by carefully sequenced curricula that have been organized into small steps. The instructional activities are under the control of the teacher at all times, and instruction does not vary from the prescribed sequence.

The phenomenological view of human beings believes that learning is intrinsic rather than extrinsic. The role of the teacher is to help children learn how to learn and how to make intelligent decisions about their own learning. In this approach to learning, play has an important place and the interests and abilities of the child are important in curriculum design. Different instructional methods are used with individuals or groups to accommodate learning styles. Classrooms utilizing this approach to learning often are unstructured and may be described as "open." The important point is that the child is viewed as an active learner and the teacher facilitates the learning process.

The checklist might be described as "cutting across" theories. Because it identifies child behaviors that are normally exhibited in the early years, it does not subscribe solely to the behaviorist or phenomenological models of early childhood education. Although the checklist is sequenced and can be used in a highly structured program, it is equally compatible to a more child-centered or discovery-oriented approach to classroom organization. Because of this flexibility, the checklist can also be found in a self-contained classroom led by a single teacher or in a team-teaching situation, where several teachers plan together for large groups of children.

In summary, the checklist is a framework; it provides teachers with concepts and skills that are appropriate for children in early childhood. The checklist does not prescribe how the children should learn or what the teacher's role should be in providing the learning experiences. The teaching style of the individual educator or theory adopted by the local school will be major determinants of the type of structure that will be used in the early childhood classroom. The following information provides suggestions of alternative possibilities for using the checklist in various types of classroom environments.

USING THE DEVELOPMENTAL CHECKLIST FOR IMPLEMENTATION OF LEARNING CENTERS

Teachers using a responsive or discovery approach to learning usually organize the environment into learning areas or centers. As the instructor decides what kinds of activities to set up in the centers, the checklist becomes a selection guide. For example, the Identification, Discrimination, and Classification Checklist can be used to organize materials. Thus a science or manipulative center might contain materials of several textures to provide experiences in rough and smooth (Level IV, 6), while the math center might house cuisenaire rods or sticks of various lengths for comparing heights (Level V, 11). In this situation the teacher provides activities in centers that match the developmental levels of the children; the teacher also interacts with the children as they use the materials.

The checklist can also be employed as reinforcement for teacher-led instruction. Using the checklist as a guide, the teacher designs group lessons to teach a concept and also places materials for the same objective in a center for children to work with during periods when they are involved in center activities. In a classroom where the checklist is used for individualized instruction, children alone or in groups can be directed to specific center activities that will reinforce their understanding of a particular concept.

USING THE DEVELOPMENTAL CHECKLIST FOR GROUP INSTRUCTION

One strategy for instructional management is teaching the entire class as a single group. This is the strategy used in more traditional kindergarten classrooms and child development nursery schools. In this type of situation the checklist can be used to help the teacher structure and sequence experiences for the class in an orderly progression. Again, materials and kits that are available become the resources for instruction. The checklist is the guide for designing the instructional sequence.

An alternative strategy for whole-group instruction is *mastery learning* as developed by Benjamin Bloom (1976). Bloom and his associates propose that 90 percent of the students in a classroom can achieve at a high level if instruction is presented in an appropriate manner. Inherent in the group instruction of mastery learning is the belief that some students need more time to master the learning content than others. If more time is provided for these students, then they too can master information at the same level as their peers. The mastery-learning approach is based on a carefully organized system of course and instructional objectives. The teacher analyzes the objectives to determine what level of mastery he or she desires from the students. For students who do not achieve the desired level of learning with the initial instructional experiences, the teacher correlates correctives or alternative ways of learning the objectives with the learning objectives in order to provide other routes to mastery. Some areas of the Frost Wortham Developmental Checklist can be used with the mastery-learning approach. Block and Anderson have written *Mastery Learning in Classroom Instruction* (1975) to provide teachers with a step-by-step method to designing and using the mastery-learning approach in their teaching.

USING THE DEVELOPMENTAL CHECKLIST FOR DIAGNOSTIC-PRESCRIPTIVE LEARNING

For teachers desiring to individualize or personalize instruction, the checklist can be used in a diagnostic-prescriptive approach to learning. In this method the teacher first assesses the strengths and weaknesses of the students using the checklist as the reference for assessment and then groups and instructs the children according to the results of the individual diagnoses. Once instruction is initiated, ongoing diagnosis provides continuous information on student progress and facilitates regrouping of students when necessary to provide for individual level and pacing of instruction.

Individualized instruction is based on a learning cycle. The learning cycle follows a pretest, instruction, and posttest sequence. In a learning cycle the teacher assesses the children to determine which instructional objective is needed. The children who have been determined to need that objective are grouped for instruction. After the children have had a series of instructional activities, the teacher reassesses them to determine which students need further assistance. Students who have successfully learned the objective move to another skill, while those needing additional activities remain for more experiences as needed. The cycle of instruction can be visualized on the diagram below:

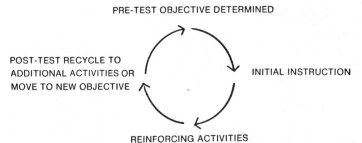

Individualized or personalized instruction also utilizes the terms *diagnosis* and *prescription* to describe how instruction meets the needs of individual learners. For each objective on the checklist requiring an activity rather than an observable behavior, the teacher has the child work with the task to determine whether that child has mastered that objective or whether the child needs to be introduced to some instructional experiences that match the objective. When the teacher has tested a series of objectives and has ascertained which objectives the child can do successfully and which need further work, diagnosis has taken place. Prescription occurs when the teacher analyzes the child's strengths and weaknesses and plans experiences that will be used with the child to extend learning to a new level.

Individualizing instruction does not imply that all directed teaching activities will be one to one. Group size will vary from one to five or more children, depending on the individual learning characteristics of the children in the classroom. The teacher will group the children for instruction based on their common needs as revealed through the diagnostic assessment. Chapters 3 through 7 will include assessments and activities for the Frost Wortham Developmental Checklist. Chapter 8 will demonstrate how the teacher can get started using a diagnostic-prescriptive approach in the classroom.

DEVELOPING A RECORDKEEPING AND RESOURCE SYSTEM
FROM THE DEVELOPMENTAL CHECKLIST

The checklist is designed to record the progress of the individual student. On the right side of the checklist are three columns where the teacher can record the results of initial and later assessment. There are several ways information can be recorded. In the example below the teacher can record the child's progress from frustration to mastery levels of performance. Either dates or " +" and "–" symbols can be used. Many teachers enter the information in pencil so that it can be altered easily.

FROST WORTHAM DEVELOPMENTAL CHECKLIST

CONCEPT DEVELOPMENT
PRESCHOOL
Identification, Discrimination, and Classification Skills
Color code: Red

LEVEL III	Frustrational	Transition	Mastery
Dates or Symbols →			
1. Discriminates between two smells	3/21		
2. Verbalizes that smells are "different"		+	
3. Discriminates between sounds and verbalizes that they are "different"			
4. Identifies sounds verbally			
5. Points to different food objects on request			
6. Discriminates differences in the shape of objects (round, square, triangular)			
7. Discriminates differences in the size of objects (big/little, long/short)			

Some teachers prefer to use other headings under which to record information. In the following example the terms *Introduced* and *Progress* are substituted for *Frustrational* and *Transition*. This form usually uses dates.

LEVEL V	Introduced	Progress	Mastery
Dates →			
3. Identifies and discriminates time relationships:			
a) morning/noon/night			
b) today/tomorrow	8/17	1/4	3/10
c) yesterday/today			
4. Labels smells verbally			
5. Identifies colors (green, orange, purple, brown, black and white)			
6. Identifies the simple properties of an object (color, shape, size)			
7. Classifies colors by intensity (dark/light, darker than/lighter than)			
8. Classifies foods (fruits, vegetables, meat)			

Although the teacher will want to maintain records for individual children, there is also the need to have a recordkeeping system for the entire class. To be able to determine which children can be grouped together for instruction, a master recordkeeping form must be devised where the progress of all the children can be followed. In order to have this kind of overall picture of class progress, the checklist must be adapted to reflect all the children in the class. An example of a master recordkeeping system of the checklist follows.

SOCIAL PLAY AND SOCIALIZING (Inter- and intrapersonal relationships, Play)

Color code: Green   Names

LEVEL III		Mary	Mario	Lisa	Henry	José	Elizabeth	Carol Ann
1.	Engages in Independent play	+	+	+	+	+	+	+
2.	Engages in parallel play	+	+	+	+	+	+	+
3.	Plays briefly with peers	+	+	+	+	+	+	+
4.	Recognizes the needs of others	+	+	+	+	+	+	+
5.	Shows sympathy for others	+	+	+	+	+	+	+
6.	Attends to an activity for ten to fifteen minutes	+	+	+	+	+	+	+
7.	Sings simple songs	+	+	+	+	+	+	+
LEVEL IV								
1.	Leaves mother readily	+	+	+	+	+	+	+
2.	Converses with other children	−	+	−	+	−	−	+
3.	Converses with adults	−	+	−	−	+	+	+
4.	Plays with peers							
5.	Cooperates in classroom routines							
6.	Takes turns and shares							
7.	Replaces materials after use	−	−	+	−	−	−	+
8.	Takes care of personal belongings							

In this example the teacher knows that two children, Lisa and Carol Ann, have demonstrated that they can use center materials appropriately (Level IV, objective 7) while Mary, Mario, Henry, José, and Elizabeth need some teacher-directed experiences in centers to help them improve their ability to return materials to shelves after they have finished using them.

As the teacher develops assessment tasks and activities for the checklist, a coding system is needed to identify and organize the activities and resources. Each part of the checklist has a color code. By adding the Roman numeral for the level and the Arabic numeral for the objective to the color code, the teacher can code any activity or resource material to the checklist. Teachers often use round, colored, stick-on labels or a marking pen to indicate the color. The color codes for the Frost Wortham Developmental Checklist are as follows:

Category	Color Code
Identification, Discrimination, and Classification	Red
Quantitative and Problem Solving	Orange
Oral Language	Brown
Reading Readiness	Yellow
Dramatic Play	Purple
Social Play and Socializing	Green
Motor Development	Blue

Below is an example of how an activity or resource material can be coded to checklist objectives. The concept to be coded is "Counts by rote from 1 to 5." Because the objective is part of the math checklist, materials used are coded orange.

FROST WORTHAM DEVELOPMENTAL CHECKLIST

CONCEPT DEVELOPMENT
Math: Quantitative and Problem Solving
Color code: Orange

LEVEL III	Frustrational	Transition	Mastery
1. Manipulates and experiments with simple machines			
2. Counts by rote from 1 to 5			

In Chapters 3 through 7 assessment tasks and activities are coded using this system to correlate with the Frost Wortham Developmental Checklist.

SUMMARY

Teachers of young children are challenged to provide optimal learning opportunities for their students. In addition to current research, which constantly adds to their knowledge of how children grow and learn, teachers can also draw from contributions made by educators, philosophers, and psychologists who have attempted to describe young children and their needs since the seventeenth century.

In the twentieth century the child-study movement initiated psychological theories of child development that described development and learning from various perspectives. During the 1950s and 1960s newer psychological theories of development and social events produced more perspectives on the early childhood years for learning. Jerome Bruner, Benjamin Bloom, Jean Piaget, and many others have contributed to an emphasis on learning potential and competencies of young children. Social awareness brought to light the special needs of low-income children. To give these children an early start on learning, the Head Start program was established, hopefully to enable them to compete better academically with their more advantaged peers.

Head Start models were based on various psychological theories of learning. The many models could be classified either as behaviorist, following Skinner's behavior analysis theory of learning, or phenomenological, using Piaget's cognitive theory of development. Each model attempted to implement a theory or combination of theories in an instructional program that would enhance learning in the early childhood years.

Educational settings today have benefit from the examples set by the Head Start models. Although theorists and resulting models do not all agree on how children develop and learn, teachers can adapt their methods to contemporary learning environments.

Because the Head Start models described goals and objectives based on commonly accepted norms of behavior for young children, educational programs today use similar objectives as a framework for their instruction with young children. The Frost Wortham Development Checklist provides a system of checklists covering all categories of development that teachers can use for educational planning and implementation in their individual school or center.

The checklist does not adhere to any one theory, thus allowing teachers to use the checklist in various ways. Teachers who are comfortable in a more structured environment and follow the behaviorist theory might utilize checklist objectives for a teacher-directed, sequential organization of instruction. Teachers who follow Piaget's child-initiated learning approach could use the same checklists to provide activities that would expose children to exploration and experimentation appropriate for their level of development. Teachers following the phenomenological view embrace the philosophy that Piagetian learning stages cannot be taught; therefore, they would use the checklist not as a director of learning but as a reference in their role as facilitator as they select materials for experiences in the learning centers. Finally, teachers interested in providing individualized instruction would find the checklist useful for diagnostic and prescriptive assessment and instruction. Whatever the teacher's philosophy, it should be remembered that checklist items derived from Piagetian theory are not intended for formal instruction.

The checklist also serves as a framework for organizing instruction. Recordkeeping systems can be devised to record children's progress individually and as a group. Curriculum materials can be identified and labeled using a coding system. Teacher-designed activities, which can be used either for assessing checklist objectives or as learning activities to be implemented within various teaching approaches, can be correlated with checklist objectives.

FROST WORTHAM DEVELOPMENTAL CHECKLIST

CONCEPT DEVELOPMENT
*PRESCHOOL**
Identification, Discrimination, and Classification Skills
Color code: Red

LEVEL III	Introduced	Progress	Mastery
1. Discriminates between two smells			
2. Verbalizes that smells are "different"			
3. Discriminates between sounds and verbalizes that they are "different"			
4. Identifies sounds verbally			
5. Points to different food objects on request			
6. Discriminates differences in the shape of objects (round, square, triangular)			
7. Discriminates differences in the size of objects (big/little, long/short)			
8. Classifies objects by weight (heavy/light)			
9. Classifies objects by height (tall/short)			
LEVEL IV			
1. Points to basic shapes (circle, square, rectangle, triangle) on request			
2. Names basic shapes:			

FROST WORTHAM DEVELOPMENTAL CHECKLIST (continued)

	Introduced	Progress	Mastery
a) circle			
b) square			
c) triangle			
d) rectangle			
3. Labels tastes verbally			
4. Identifies primary colors (red, yellow, blue)			
5. Identifies likenesses and differences in two or more objects (shape, size, color)			
6. Discriminates differences (opposites) in:			
a) sound (loud/soft)			
b) amount (full/empty)			
c) texture (rough/smooth, hard/soft)			
7. Identifies spatial relationships:			
a) far/near			
b) in/out			
c) front/back			
d) high/low			
8. Identifies and discriminates time relationships:			
a) before/after			
b) earlier/later			
9. Identifies and discriminates actions:			
a) run			
b) walk			
c) jump			
10. Classifies objects by more than one property			
11. Reverses simple operations:			
a) stacks/unstacks/restacks			
b) arranges/disarranges/rearranges			
12. Classifies by condition:			
a) hot/cold			
b) wet/dry			
13. Identifies and discriminates value relationships:			
a) right/wrong			
b) good/bad			
c) pretty/ugly			
d) sad/happy			

LEVEL V

1. Identifies spatial relationships:
   a) top/bottom

FROST WORTHAM DEVELOPMENTAL CHECKLIST (continued)

	Introduced	Progress	Mastery
b) over/under			
2. Identifies and discriminates value relationships (like/dislike)			
3. Identifies and discriminates time relationships:			
a) morning/noon/night			
b) today/tomorrow			
c) yesterday/today			
4. Labels smells verbally			
5. Identifies colors (green, orange, purple, brown, black and white)			
6. Identifies the simple properties of an object (color, shape, size)			
7. Classifies colors by intensity (dark/light, darker than/lighter than)			
8. Classifies foods (fruits, vegetables, meat)			
9. Classifies tastes (sweet, sour, salty)			
10. Classifies surfaces by textures (smooth, rough, soft, hard)			
11. Identifies and classifies common objects by shape (circle, rectangle, triangle, oval, square)			
12. Seriates (arranges) objects by size			
13. Classifies by function:			
a) food/eat			
b) vehicle/ride			

*Developed by Joe Frost and Sue Wortham; revised and validated July 1980. Used by permission of Joe L. Frost.

FROST WORTHAM DEVELOPMENTAL CHECKLIST

CONCEPT DEVELOPMENT
PRESCHOOL*
Math: Quantitative and Problem Solving
Color code: Orange

LEVEL III	Introduced	Progress	Mastery
1. Manipulates and experiments with simple machines			
2. Counts by rote from 1 to 5			
3. Forms creative designs with materials			
4. Uses construction materials for multiple purposes			
5. Perceives objects from different visual perspectives			
LEVEL IV			
1. Counts by rote from 1 to 10			
2. Demonstrates the concept of number through 5			
3. Orders the numerals 1 to 5			
4. Understands the concepts of *first* and *last*			
5. Identifies:			
a) penny			
b) nickel			
c) dime			
6. Compares differences in dimension (taller/shorter, longer/shorter, thinner/wider)			
7. Demonstrates one-to-one correspondence			
LEVEL V			
1. Counts to 50			
2. Demonstrates the concept of numbers through 10			
3. Orders the numerals 1 to 10			
4. Writes numerals for sets 1 to 10			
5. Identifies pairs of familiar objects (shoes, socks, gloves, earrings)			
6. Groups objects into sets of equal number			
7. Compares elements of unequal sets (more than/fewer than)			
8. Combines (adds) the total number in two small groups			
9. Uses ordinal concepts up through *third*			

FROST WORTHAM DEVELOPMENTAL CHECKLIST (continued)

	Introduced	Progress	Mastery
10. Identifies:			
a) penny			
b) nickel			
c) dime			
d) quarter			
11. Compares distance (height, width) to an independent object			
12. Compares volumes in separate containers			
13. Tells time to the hour			

*Developed by Joe Frost and Sue Wortham; revised and validated, July 1980. Used by permission of Joe L. Frost.

FROST WORTHAM DEVELOPMENTAL CHECKLIST

*LANGUAGE DEVELOPMENT**
Oral Language

Color code: Brown

LEVEL III	Introduced	Progress	Mastery
1. Produces language that is mostly intelligible			
2. Recognizes and verbally labels common objects			
3. Responds correctly to simple instructions involving locations in the classroom			
4. Uses sentences of four to five words			
5. Asks questions to gain problem-solving information			
LEVEL IV			
1. Uses simple position words such as *over* and *under*			
2. Uses simple action words such as *run* and *walk*			
3. Uses complete sentences			
4. Uses language for specific purposes (directions, information)			
5. Verbalizes routine events ("We're going out to play")			
6. Averages five-word sentences			
7. Follows simple sentences			
8. Repeats nursery rhymes			

FROST WORTHAM DEVELOPMENTAL CHECKLIST (continued)

	Introduced	Progress	Mastery
LEVEL V			
1. Communicates ideas, feelings, and emotions in well-formed sentences			
2. Uses the correct form of more verbs in informal conversation			
3. Uses the correct prepositions to denote place and position			
4. Uses most personal pronouns correctly			
5. Explains the operation of simple machines			
6. Uses language to get what she or he wants			
7. Can follow instructions containing three parts			

*Developed by Joe Frost and Sue Wortham. Used by permission of Joe L. Frost.

FROST WORTHAM DEVELOPMENTAL CHECKLIST

*LANGUAGE DEVELOPMENT**
Reading Readiness

Color code: Yellow

LEVEL V	Introduced	Progress	Mastery
Auditory Discrimination			
1. Discriminates between similar sounds made by different objects			
2. Discriminates between initial phonemes (*bat/cat, fat/rat, plat/flat, sat/hat, fan/Dan*)			
3. Discriminates between medial phonemes (*bet/bit, bat/but, bit/bat, bin/ban, hot/hat*)			
4. Discriminates between final phonemes (*bat/bam, can/cad, bet/bed*)			
Visual Discrimination			
5. Discriminates likenesses and differences in pictured objects, shapes, letters, and words			
6. Uses visual memory to match pictured objects, shapes, letters, and words with one removed			
7. Identifies his or her first name in print			

FROST WORTHAM DEVELOPMENTAL CHECKLIST (continued)

	Introduced	Progress	Mastery
8. Tracks visually from left to right			
9. Follows left-to-right progression of a pointer while an adult reads			
Letter Knowledge			
10. Matches upper- and lower-case letters			
11. Identifies the letters of the alphabet			
12. Arranges letters in alphabetical order			
13. Matches letters with pictures of objects whose names begin with the same sound as the letter			
Language and Vocabulary			
14. Listens to and follows verbal directions			
15. Identifies the concept of word			
16. Identifies the concept of letter			
17. Invents a story for a picture book			
Oral Comprehension			
18. Locates elements in a picture (tallest, largest, and so forth)			
19. Retells in the correct sequence a story read to him or her			
20. Reorganizes pictures to show the correct story sequence			
21. Answers recall questions about a story			
22. Draws analogies from a story to his or her own experience			
23. Makes value judgments about story events			
Experience Chart Skills			
24. Tells experiences for an experience story			
25. Follows left-to-right progression as an adult reads			
26. Identifies recurring words on an experience chart			
27. Suggests titles for experience stories			
Fine Motor			
28. Draws circles with closed ends			
29. Connects dots with straight pencil lines			
30. Copies shapes from a model			
31. Copies alphabet letters from a model			

*Developed by Joe Frost and Sue Wortham. Used by permission of Joe L. Frost.

FROST WORTHAM DEVELOPMENTAL CHECKLIST

DRAMATIC PLAY
*PRESCHOOL**

Color code: Purple

LEVEL III

	Introduced	Progress	Mastery
1. Imitates grownups (plays house, store, and so forth)			
2. Expresses frustrations in play			
3. Creates imaginary playmates			
4. Engages in housekeeping			
5. Paints and draws symbolic figures on large paper			
6. Builds simple structures with blocks			
7. Uses transportation toys, people, and animals to enrich block play			
8. Imagines any object as the object he or she wants (symbolic function)			

LEVEL IV

	Introduced	Progress	Mastery
1. Role plays in the housekeeping center			
2. Role plays some adult occupations			
3. Participates in dramatization of familiar stories			
4. Uses puppets in self-initiated dialogues			
5. Differentiates between real and make-believe			
6. Pretends dolls are real people			
7. Constructs (paints, molds, and so forth) recognizable figures			
8. Participates in finger plays			

LEVEL V

	Introduced	Progress	Mastery
1. Role plays a wide variety of roles in the housekeeping center and in other centers.			
2. Role plays on the playground			
3. Role plays a variety of adult occupations			
4. Recognizes that pictures represent real objects			
5. Participates in a wide variety of creative activities: finger plays, rhythm band, working with clay, painting, outdoor play, housekeeping, singing, and so forth			
6. Produces objects at the carpentry table and tells about them			

FROST WORTHAM DEVELOPMENTAL CHECKLIST (continued)

	Introduced	Progress	Mastery
7. Produces art objects and tells about them			
8. Searches for better ways to construct			
9. Builds complex block structures			

*Developed by Joe Frost and Sue Wortham. Used by permission of Joe L. Frost.

FROST WORTHAM DEVELOPMENTAL CHECKLIST

SOCIAL PLAY AND SOCIALIZING PRESCHOOL*

Color code: Green

LEVEL III	Introduced	Progress	Mastery
1. Engages in independent play			
2. Engages in parallel play			
3. Plays briefly with peers			
4. Recognizes the needs of others			
5. Shows sympathy for others			
6. Attends to an activity for ten to fifteen minutes			
7. Sings simple songs			

LEVEL IV			
1. Leaves the mother readily			
2. Converses with other children			
3. Converses with adults			
4. Plays with peers			
5. Cooperates in classroom routines			
6. Takes turns and shares			
7. Replaces materials after use			
8. Takes care of personal belongings			
9. Respects the property of others			
10. Attends to an activity for fifteen to twenty minutes			
11. Engages in group activities			
12. Sings with a group			
13. Is sensitive to praise and criticism			

FROST WORTHAM DEVELOPMENTAL CHECKLIST (continued)

LEVEL V	Introduced	Progress	Mastery
1. Completes most self-initiated projects			
2. Works and plays with limited supervision			
3. Engages in cooperative play			
4. Listens while peers speak			
5. Follows multiple and delayed directions			
6. Carries out special responsibilities (for example, feeding animals)			
7. Listens and follows the suggestions of adults			
8. Enjoys talking with adults			
9. Can sustain an attention span for a variety of duties			
10. Evaluates his or her work and suggests improvements			

*Developed by Joe Frost and Sue Wortham. Used by permission of Joe L. Frost.

FROST WORTHAM DEVELOPMENTAL CHECKLIST

*MOTOR DEVELOPMENT PRESCHOOL**
Gross Movement

Color code: Blue

LEVEL III	Introduced	Progress	Mastery
1. Catches a ball with both hands against the chest			
2. Rides a tricycle			
3. Hops on both feet several times without assistance			
4. Throws a ball five feet with accuracy			
5. Climbs up a slide and comes down			
6. Climbs by alternating feet and holding on to a handrail			
7. Stands on one foot and balances briefly			
8. Pushes a loaded wheelbarrow			
9. Runs freely with little stumbling or falling			
10. Builds a tower with nine or ten blocks			

FROST WORTHAM DEVELOPMENTAL CHECKLIST (continued)

	Introduced	Progress	Mastery
LEVEL IV			
1. Balances on one foot			
2. Walks a straight line forward and backward			
3. Walks a balance beam			
4. Climbs steps with alternate feet without support			
5. Climbs on a jungle gym			
6. Skips haltingly			
7. Throws, catches, and bounces a large ball			
8. Stacks blocks vertically and horizontally			
9. Creates recognizable block structures			
10. Rides a tricycle with speed and skill			
LEVEL V			
1. Catches and throws a small ball			
2. Bounces and catches a small ball			
3. Skips on either foot			
4. Skips rope			
5. Hops on one foot			
6. Creates Tinkertoy and block structures			
7. Hammers and saws with some skill			
8. Walks a balance beam forward and backward			
9. Descends stairs by alternating feet			

*Developed by Joe Frost and Sue Wortham. Used by permission of Joe L. Frost.

FROST WORTHAM DEVELOPMENTAL CHECKLIST

MOTOR DEVELOPMENT
*PRESCHOOL**
Fine Movement

Color code: Blue

	Introduced	Progress	Mastery
LEVEL III			
1. Places small pegs in pegboards			
2. Holds a paintbrush or pencil with the whole hand			

FROST WORTHAM DEVELOPMENTAL CHECKLIST (continued)

	Introduced	Progress	Mastery
3. Eats with a spoon			
4. Buttons large buttons on his or her own clothes			
5. Puts on coat unassisted			
6. Strings bead with ease			
7. Hammers a pound toy with accuracy			
8. Works a three- or four-piece puzzle			
LEVEL IV			
1. Pounds and rolls clay			
2. Puts together a five-piece puzzle			
3. Forms a pegboard design			
4. Cuts with scissors haltingly and pastes			
5. Eats with a fork correctly			
6. Holds a cup with one hand			
7. Puts a coat on a hanger or hook			
8. Manipulates large crayons and brushes			
9. Buttons buttons and zips zippers haltingly			
LEVEL V			
1. Cuts and pastes creative designs			
2. Forms a variety of pegboard designs			
3. Buttons buttons, zips zippers, and ties shoes			
4. Creates recognizable objects with clay			
5. Uses the toilets independently			
6. Eats independently with a knife and fork			
7. Dresses and undresses independently			
8. Holds and manipulates pencils, crayons, and brushes of various sizes			
9. Combs and brushes hair			
10. Works a twelve-piece puzzle			

*Developed by Joe Frost and Sue Wortham. Used by permission of Joe L. Frost.

REFERENCES

Block, J., and Anderson, L. *Mastery Learning in Classroom Instruction.* New York: Macmillan, 1975.

Bloom, B. *Stability and Change in Human Characteristics.* New York: Wiley, 1964.

Bloom, B. *Human Characteristics and School Learning.* New York: McGraw-Hill, 1976.

Bruner, J. *The Process of Education*. Washington, D.C.: Howard University Press, 1960.

Bushell, Jr., D. "The Behavior Analysis Model for Early Education." In B. Spodek (ed.). *Research in Early Childhood Education*. New York: Free Press, 1982.

Erikson, E. *Childhood and Society*. New York: Norton, 1950.

Freud, S. *The Basic Writings of Sigmund Freud* (Translated and edited by A. A. Brill). New York: Random House, 1938.

Gesell, A. "The Ontogenesis of Infant Behavior." In L. Carmichael (ed.). *Manual of Child Psychology*. New York: Wiley, 1954.

Hall, G. S. *Youth*. New York: D. Appleton, 1906.

Hitt, W. "Two Models of Man." *American Psychologist* 24, no. 7 (July 1969): 651–658.

Hohmann, M.; Banet, B.; and Weikart, D. *Young Children in Action: A Handbook for Preschool Educators*. Ypsilanti, Mich.: High Scope Press, 1979.

Piaget, J. *The Origins of Intelligence in Children*. New York: International University Press, 1952.

Ransbury, M. K. "Frederick Froebel, 1782–1982: A Reexamination of Froebel's Principles of Childhood Learning." *Childhood Education* 59, no. 2 (1982): 104–106.

Sharp, E. *Thinking Is Child's Play*. New York: Avon Books, 1969.

Skinner, B.F. *Science and Human Behavior*. New York: Free Press, 1953.

Spodek, B. *Early Childhood Education*. Englewood Cliffs, N.J.: Prentice-Hall, 1973.

Wellman, H. M. "The Foundations of Knowledge: Concept Development in Young Children." In S. G. Moore and C. R. Cooper (eds.). *The Young Child Reviews of Research, Volume 3*. Washington, D.C.: National Association for the Education of Young Children, 1982.

CHAPTER **3**

Identification, Discrimination, and Classification Skills

During the years of early childhood, children are at what Piaget calls the preoperational stage of development. Because they think and learn differently than adults, it is helpful to know the characteristics of their learning as they mature. This chapter is concerned with the cognitive development of the child and the related checklist titled Identification, Discrimination, and Classification Skills. The objectives of the checklist are explained, followed by activities designed to meet checklist objectives.

HOW CHILDREN DEVELOP CONCEPTS

The ability to think is a vehicle by which the young child learns. The acquisition of concepts is the process through which the child uses thinking to expand his or her knowledge of the world. The changes in knowledge and thinking skills and the way they are organized and used in dealing with problems explain cognitive development (Copple, DeLisi, and Sigel, 1982).

Wellman (1982) defines concepts as cognitive categories used to group together events or items using perceptually distinct information. Individual concepts are grouped together into conceptual systems. Wellman divides concepts into two overlapping sets: concepts of the physical world and concepts of the social world. Curriculum areas such as mathematics, science, music, and art relate to the physical world, while social studies, affective education, moral education, and multicultural education are part of the social world.

The young child does not possess all of the concepts and categories of concepts, but acquires them gradually during growth. The development of the ability to think and to understand that others also think occurs in the preoperational period. When Piaget studied the development of dreams and thought (1929), he determined that preschoolers at first identify mental events with behaviors. That is, the child is unable to understand that mental processes are unobservable. Two and three year olds are beginning to form concepts of thinking when they use words such as *remember* and *think* in their language. Four and five year olds not only understand that people think differently from each other but are able to use many mental terms in their speech.

These observations demonstrate a definite relationship between language and cognition. Piaget (1952) proposed that language is a subset of cognitive and symbolic functioning. On the other hand, Vygotsky (1962) believed that higher levels of cognition originated in language. Prutting (1979) also argued that the development of linguistic behavior derives from the cognitive processes present in the child at various stages of development. Regardless of which position is taken—language before cognitive development or cognitive development before language—the two areas of development are related, and they facilitate each other in a complementary manner.

The preoperational child is in the process of developing language and concepts through personal action on, interaction with, and reaction to objects, events, people, and ideas (Thibault and McKee, 1982). The child, as characterized by Hohmann, Banet, and Weikart (1979), is an *active* learner.

As was discussed in Chapter 2, the preoperational child is intuitive and egocentric. Piaget (1952) subdivided the preoperational stage into the egocentric period (two to four years) and the intuitive phase (four to seven years). During the egocentric period the child uses language for representation. The child can now engage in problem solving using verbalization with others. However, the egocentric child still thinks that everyone has the same thoughts.

In the intuitive phase the child can engage in simple classifying. Reversibility and conservation are not yet achieved because the child centers or focuses on one aspect of a problem at a time. Reversibility means the child understands that what is assembled or arranged can be disassembled or rearranged. Children achieve conservation when they are able to demonstrate an understanding of the constancy of matter when the shape or location is changed.

The preoperational child can discriminate by size. Although the child cannot yet conserve, she or he does understand seriation. The ability to make one-to-one correspondences also develops during this period.

IMPLICATIONS FOR EDUCATION

Wellman (1982) contrasts possibilities about how children learn, passively or actively. If the child is thought of as a passive learner, the parent serves as a trainer. Conversely, Piaget would describe the child as an active seeker and interpreter of information in concept development. The role of the parents and teacher is to provide experiences that will stimulate concept development. Adult support and direction enhances the possibilities that the child will use ongoing active learning to develop the concepts necessary for later learning.

Hohmann, Banet, and Weikart (1979) describe the role of the adult as that of being an instigator of problem-solving activities in cognitive development. They suggest that the adult can serve as a facilitator of learning by:

1. Providing a rich array of materials and activities from which children are invited to select.
2. Explicitly asking children to plan, in some way, what they are going to do and how they are going to do it. This permits children to begin to set goals for themselves and to generate and evaluate alternative solutions to problems en route to achieving the goals.
3. Asking questions and making suggestions in order to set the stage for key experiences that stimulate the child's thinking processes, language development, and social development (p. 6).

USING THE IDENTIFICATION, DISCRIMINATION, AND CLASSIFICATION SKILLS CHECKLIST

The broad categories of identification, discrimination, and classification skills include many kinds of concepts. Because language is an integral part of concept development, vocabulary is a part of some identification skills.

The checklist treats the areas of concept development in levels of complexity. *Identification*, or naming, is the simplest level of understanding. *Discrimination* involves comparison of items in a category according to a physical dimension such as size or weight. Seriation, the ordering of objects by a physical dimension, is one type of discrimination. *Classification*, the most complex operation, requires the ability to group objects by a common characteristic or characteristics. The tasks at each level of the checklist require higher developmental skills. The meaning of each objective, including its level of complexity, is explained in the material following the checklist. The teacher should remember that objectives related to Piagetian tasks are not meant to be taught; rather, they are to be used to provide experiences and to assess progress in development.

FROST WORTHAM DEVELOPMENTAL CHECKLIST

CONCEPT DEVELOPMENT
PRESCHOOL*
Identification, Discrimination, and Classification Skills
Color code: Red

	Introduced	Progress	Mastery
LEVEL III			
1. Discriminates between two smells			
2. Verbalizes that smells are "different"			
3. Discriminates between sounds and verbalizes that they are "different"			
4. Identifies sounds verbally			
5. Points to different food objects on request			
6. Discriminates differences in the shape of objects (round, square, triangular)			
7. Discriminates differences in the size of objects (big/little, long/short)			
8. Classifies objects by weight (heavy/light)			
9. Classifies objects by height (tall/short)			
LEVEL IV			
1. Points to basic shapes (circle, square, rectangle, triangle) on request			
2. Names basic shapes:			
a) circle			
b) square			
c) triangle			
d) rectangle			
3. Labels tastes verbally			
4. Identifies primary colors (red, yellow, blue)			
5. Identifies likenesses and differences in two or more objects (shape, size, color)			
6. Discriminates differences (opposites) in:			
a) sound (loud/soft)			
b) amount (full/empty)			
c) texture (rough/smooth, hard/soft)			
7. Identies spatial relationships:			
a) far/near			
b) in/out			
c) front/back			

FROST WORTHAM DEVELOPMENTAL CHECKLIST (continued)

	Introduced	Progress	Mastery
d) high/low			
8. Identifies and discriminates time relationships:			
a) before/after			
b) earlier/later			
9. Identifies and discriminates actions:			
a) run			
b) walk			
c) jump			
10. Classifies objects by more than one property			
11. Reverses simple operations:			
a) stacks/unstacks/restacks			
b) arranges/disarranges/rearranges			
12. Classifies by condition:			
a) hot/cold			
b) wet/dry			
c) old/new			
13. Identifies and discriminates value relationships:			
a) right/wrong			
b) good/bad			
c) pretty/ugly			
d) sad/happy			
LEVEL V			
1. Identifies spatial relationships:			
a) top/bottom			
b) over/under			
2. Identifies and discriminates value relationships (like/dislike)			
3. Identifies and discriminates time relationships:			
a) morning/noon/night			
b) today/tomorrow			
c) yesterday/today			
4. Labels smells verbally			
5. Identifies colors (green, orange, purple, brown, black and white)			
6. Identifies the simple properties of an object (color, shape, size)			
7. Classifies colors by intensity (dark/light, darker/lighter)			
8. Classifies foods (fruits, vegetables, meat)			

FROST WORTHAM DEVELOPMENTAL CHECKLIST (continued)

	Introduced	Progress	Mastery
9. Classifies tastes (sweet, sour, salty)			
10. Classifies surfaces by textures (smooth, rough, soft, hard)			
11. Identifies and classifies common objects by shape (circle, rectangle, triangle, oval, square)			
12. Seriates (arranges) objects by size			
13. Classifies by function:			
a) food/eat			
b) vehicle/ride			

*Developed by Joe Frost and Sue Wortham; revised and validated July 1980. Used by permission of Joe L. Frost.

FROST WORTHAM DEVELOPMENTAL CHECKLIST
IDENTIFICATION, DISCRIMINATION, AND CLASSIFICATION SKILLS

LEVEL III

1. *Discriminates between two smells*
    In this objective the child is presented with two smells that the teacher has placed in several containers. On request the child indicates by pointing when two containers smell the "same" or "not the same." The child is learning the concepts of same and different but is not required to verbalize.

2. *Verbalizes that smells are "different"*
    At this level the child is asked, not only to discriminate between two smells, but also to verbalize differences. In presenting smells the teacher asks the child to select smells that are the "same" or "different." As a second step the teacher selects two containers and asks the child to determine whether the smells are the "same" or "different."

3.. *Discriminates between sounds and verbalizes that they are "different"*
    As in discrimination of smells, sounds are presented, such as those that result from tapping rhythm sticks or ringing a bell. The teacher may present two like sounds or different sounds. First the teacher asks the child to indicate when two sounds presented are the "same" or "different." Then the teacher asks the child to label the sounds as "same" or "different."

4. *Identifies sounds verbally*
    Given common sounds such as those from a piano, bell, door closing, and so on, the child is able to identify the sound. Recordings of common sounds are also available.

5. *Points to different food objects on request*
    The teacher presents common food items by categories, such as fruits or vegetables. As the teacher names the items, the child is able to point to the item named.
6. *Discriminates differences in the shape of objects (round, square, triangular)*
    The teacher presents objects such as a ball, box, block, and so on. The child is able to identify whether the objects are the same or different in shape. At a simpler level the teacher can present an array of shapes and ask the child to determine whether two pieces in particular are alike or different in shape.
7. *Discriminates differences in the size of objects (big/little, long/short)*
    The child is able to differentiate sizes presented by the teacher. The teacher asks questions such as, ''Show me the big car.'' The child does not have to verbalize but is able to point to the correct item, using size when questioned by the teacher.
8. *Classifies objects by weight (heavy/light)*
    Given an array of objects that are obviously different in weight, the child is able to separate them into two groups labeled ''heavy'' and ''light.'' The teacher identifies the two groups for the child. Examples of objects that can be used are a cotton ball, a feather, a piece of fabric, a rock, a ball bearing, and a paperweight.
9. *Classifies objects by height (tall/short)*
    As in objective 8, the teacher presents items of obviously different lengths to the child. The child is asked to separate the items into two groups according to whether they are tall and short.

LEVEL IV

1. *Points to basic shapes (circle, square, rectangle, triangle) on request*
    The teacher presents the basic shapes. The child is able to point to the shape when it is named by the teacher. As with other similar objectives at this level, the child identifies the shape by pointing but need not give the name of the shape.
2. *Names basic shapes: circle; square; triangle; rectangle*
    This objective is the next level of difficulty from objective 1. The child demonstrates knowledge of the shapes by naming them when they are presented.
3. *Labels tastes verbally*
    The teacher presents the child with common food items to taste, such as peanut butter, banana, orange, and so on. The child is able to name the tasted food. The teacher should be sure that the food items are familiar to the child.
4. *Identifies primary colors (red, yellow, blue)*
    When presented with items in the primary colors, the child is able to name which items are red, which yellow, and which blue.

5. *Identifies likenesses and differences in two or more objects (shape, size, color)*
    Given an array of objects that are different in shape, size, and color, the child can verbalize whether any two items are the same or different in a particular characteristic. Objects such as balls and cubes that have characteristics in common as well as differences may be used.

6. *Discriminates differences (opposites) in: sound (loud/soft); amount (full/ empty); texture (rough/smooth, hard/soft)*
    The teacher shows the child an array of objects and picks a category of opposites. The child then identifies the opposites by choosing items from the given array. The child will have to understand the meaning of *opposite* in addition to identifying the appropriate item. For *full* and *empty* the teacher shows the child two containers, one of which is full and the other empty. The child is asked to point to the full container. Similar activities can be used for the other contrasting pairs. As in other categories, only one concept pair should be used at a time when taught for the first time.

7. *Identifies spatial relationships: far/near; in/out; front/back; high/low*
    These concepts can also be assessed through discussions using objects in various positions or through activities using the child or children. The teacher may ask the child to place items in various positions in relationship to another item. Or the teacher may ask the child to identify where an object is in relationship to another object. As an alternative, children may be asked to carry out commands that involve spatial relationships. For example, the teacher may ask, "Please get in front of the desk," and the child carries out the command.

8. *Identifies and discriminates time relationships: before/after; earlier/later*
    Through questions and discussions of a sequence of verbal or pictured events, the teacher asks the child to identify the time relationship. Using two pictures the teacher may ask the child to determine which event happened earlier and which happened later. To assess knowledge of time, the teacher may ask in a discussion, "Do you take a nap before lunch or after lunch?"

9. *Identifies and discriminates actions: run; walk; jump*
    The discriminations of actions may be determined by having the child engage in the actions on command. The child may also identify the actions by watching another child using them or by identifying the action in a picture.

10. *Classifies objects by more than one property*
    The child is presented with an array of items that vary in more than one property, such as color or size. The teacher asks the child to divide the items into two groups. After the classification is completed, the next task is to regroup the items using another kind of classification. For example, a collection of books could be classified by thickness and then size, or by size and then color.

11. *Reverses simple operations: stacks/unstacks/restacks; arranges/disarranges/ rearranges*

The child is able to demonstrate that an operation can be reversed. The teacher constructs an arrangement or pattern of items and then asks the child to mix up the items and reconstruct the pattern. As an alternative the teacher may ask the child to make an arrangement of objects, destroy the arrangement, and then rebuild the original arrangement.

12. *Classifies by condition: hot/cold; wet/dry; old/new*
    Given an array of items, the child is asked to classify the items by category. Real items are best; however, pictures of hot and cold foods, for example, may be used. It is relatively easy to collect old and new items to be compared.

13. *Identifies and discriminates value relationships: right/wrong; good/bad; pretty/ugly; sad/happy*
    These concepts may be evaluated through discussions or through the use of pictures. The teacher asks the child to make value judgments about situations presented verbally or pictorially. A picture of a broken window may elicit opinions regarding how the window was broken and whether the actions that caused the window to be broken are good or bad. Likewise, a picture of a littered piece of property may be discussed in terms of ''pretty'' and ''ugly.'' The teacher must be accepting of the child's values, which might be different from the teacher's own, since a teacher's perspective can differ greatly from a child's point of view.

LEVEL V

1. *Identifies spatial relationships: top/bottom; over/under*
   This objective is the same as Level IV, objective 7. It may be assessed by asking the child to locate items or follow commands using his or her body or using play objects. For example, the teacher may ask the child ''Bring the book from the top shelf.''

2. *Identifies and discriminates value relationships: like/dislike*
   Children at this level are more likely to understand the concept of *like* before understanding *dislike*. To understand these value relationships the child needs to have experiences that involve the use of the two terms in a meaningful context. For example, children can discuss foods they like and do not like. One assessment activity might be to have the children volunteer things they like and dislike within a category such as clothing, restaurants, and so on.

3. *Identifies and discriminates time relationships: morning/noon/night; today/ tomorrow; yesterday/today*
   These time concepts are abstract. The child's understanding of time can be determined by discussing the day's events. The teacher makes the statement ''We get up in the _____'' and then asks the child to make the correct response. Another method is to collect pictures that depict times such as morning and night and then to ask the child to

identify what part of the day is being depicted using clues given in the picture. A discussion of events may also be used for *today* and *tomorrow*. The question "Will we go to the grocery store today or tomorrow?" gives indications of the child's understanding of these time categories.

4. *Labels smells verbally*
   When presented with common smells, the child is able to identify them. Some examples are perfume, onion, and orange juice.

5. *Identifies colors (green, orange, purple, brown, black and white)*
   As with the procedure for naming the primary colors, the teacher presents the child with an array of colors and asks the child to find and point to the named color. At a higher level the teacher points to the color and asks the child to give the name of the color.

6. *Identifies the simple properties of an object (color, shape, size)*
   This objective requires the child to understand the meaning of color, shape, and size and to be able to verbalize them in describing the object. Given an array of shapes of various colors and sizes, the child is able to follow the direction of the teacher. The teacher may say, "When we say the triangle is green, we are talking about its _____." Another example is, "Circles, triangles and squares are all called _____." The child is expected to complete the statement correctly. Another method of assessing understanding of properties is for the teacher to select an item and ask the child to describe the color, shape, and size of the object.

7. *Classifies colors by intensity (dark/light, darker than/lighter than)*
   The teacher gives the child an array of colors that have different shades. At first the child is asked to make groups of items that are dark or light. The next step is for the child to identify colors that are darker than or lighter than a given color.

8. *Classifies foods (fruits, vegetables, meat)*
   The teacher gives the child an array of items, preferably real items or three-dimensional representations. If these are not available, pictures can be used. The teacher then asks the child to group the items according to the given categories.

9. *Classifies tastes (sweet, sour, salty)*
   The teacher gives the child items of food in each taste category. The child samples each item and identifies the category to which it belongs as the teacher names the categories.

10. *Classifies surfaces by texture (smooth, rough, soft, hard)*
    The teacher presents the child with an array of objects that have the four textures named. The child is asked to separate the items into groups and identify each category.

11. *Identifies and classifies common objects by shape (circle, rectangle, triangle, oval, square)*
    Given an array of two- and three-dimensional shapes, the child, when

asked, separates the objects into groups by shape and identifies the shape category for each group.

12. *Seriates (arranges) objects by size*
The teacher gives the child a group of objects that vary in length or size. The child then puts the objects in order from small to large or from long to short. Dowels that have been cut into segments of various lengths are one example of items that may be used.

13. *Classifies by function: food/eat; vehicle/ride*
The teacher gives the child an array of pictures or objects that belong to several categories. From the array the child groups all the items that are to eat, for example. The child must also be able to identify the category or class. Many categories, such as tools and toys, may be used for classification.

IDENTIFICATION, DISCRIMINATION, AND CLASSIFICATION ACTIVITIES

The following activities are correlated to the checklist. The main purpose of the activities is to enable the teacher to provide the kinds of experiences that will enhance the development of concepts. The role of the teacher as facilitator of learning is to use discussion and questioning if the activity involves teacher guidance. Many of the identification and discrimination activities include more specific direction as the children are encouraged to include naming of attributes as part of the activity. Some of the activities do not require teacher direction but allow the child to explore and experiment in a solitary or small-group experience. The activities may be used for assessment as well as for learning experiences.

IDENTIFICATION, DISCRIMINATION, AND CLASSIFICATION SKILLS

Level III

Objective 1: Discriminates between two smells

Materials

One small can of cinnamon and one small bottle of cinnamon
One small can of thyme and one small bottle of thyme

Activity

The teacher presents the child with two smells from the cans. The teacher then places the four containers of spices on the table and asks the child to identify the sets of spices that are the same.

Group Size

Individual
Small group

Objective 2: Verbalizes that smells are "different"

Materials

Two film containers, each with a cotton ball inside. The cotton balls are dipped into different solutions such as vinegar and cherry juice.

Activity

The teacher asks the child to take the lids off, one container at a time, and sniff the smells. Next, the child determines if the smells are the same or different.

Group Size

Individual

Small group

Level III

Objective 5: Points to different food objects on request

Materials
Pictures of meats, fruits, vegetables, and bread glued on index cards

Activity
The teacher presents the cards to the children and helps them name the pictured foods. The teacher then names a food and asks the children to find it from the array of pictures. As a classification activity, the teacher asks the child to organize the pictures by category.

Group Size
Small group
Large group

Objective 6: Discriminates differences in the shape of
objects (round, square, triangular)

Materials

Legal size manila folder

Two geometric shapes cut from red, yellow, blue, and green posterboard. One set of shapes is glued to the folder. The other set of
shapes is stored in an attached envelope.

Activity

The teacher asks the child to take the colored shapes in the envelope and
place each on top of the same colored shape glued to the folder. When
the activity is completed the child will have matched the shapes as well as
the colors.

Group Size

Individual

IDENTIFICATION, DISCRIMINATION, AND CLASSIFICATION SKILLS

Level III

Objective 7: Discriminates differences in the size of objects
(big/little, long/short)

Materials
A collection of nails of different lengths

Activity
The teacher selects two nails and demonstrates for the child how they can
be compared in length as being "long" or "short." The child then selects a
long nail and a short nail. Later the child can order the nails from long to
short or vice versa.

Group Size
Individual
Small group

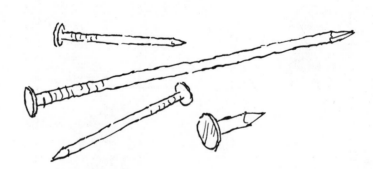

Objective 1: Points to basic shapes (circle, square, rectangle, triangle) on request

Materials
One of each of the basic shapes cut out of wood and sanded

Activity
The teacher presents the shapes to the child, naming each shape. The teacher then asks the child to point to each shape as it is named by the teacher.

Group Size
Individual
Small group

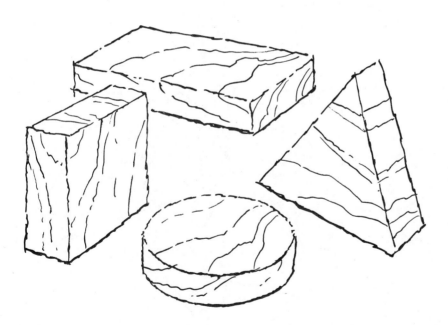

Level IV

Objective 1: Points to basic shapes (circle, square, rectangle, triangle) on request

---

Materials

An array of four shapes

Activity

The teacher presents the array of shapes to the child and names each category of shape for the child. The child then has to match a shape the teacher holds up and names. Finally, the teacher names a shape without showing it and asks the child to point to or pick up each shape as it is named.

Group Size

Individual
Small group
Large group

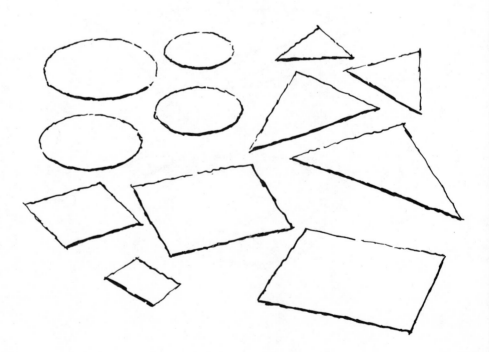

> Objective 2: Names basic shapes: circle; square; triangle;
> rectangle

Materials

Shoebox with construction paper shapes glued to the bottom
Envelope taped to the side of the shoebox
> A collection of shapes cut out of construction paper stored in the
> envelope

Activity

The child is asked to name the shapes on the bottom of the shoebox. Then
the teacher takes the shapes from the envelope. As the child names each
shape, the teacher places it on the appropriate shape in the shoebox.

Group Size

Individual

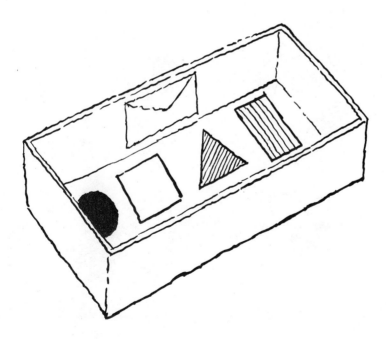

> Objective 4: Identifies primary colors (red, yellow, blue)

Materials

A collection of small toy objects in primary colors

Activity

The teacher asks the child to sort the toys by color. If the child knows the colors, the teacher may ask that they be identified. If the child does not know the colors, the teacher may identify the color of each object and then ask the child to point to a toy of a particular color.

Group Size

Individual

Small group

Objective 4: Identifies primary colors (red, yellow, blue)

Materials
Shoestring
Foam rubber rings or beads, in primary colors

Activity
After naming each primary color, the teacher asks the children to string the appropriate color bead on the string. After all colors are represented on the shoestring, the teacher asks the children to name each color and identify something in the room also of that color. Another activity is to have a child or teacher put a pattern of beads on the shoestring for the others to duplicate.

Group Size
Small group
Large group

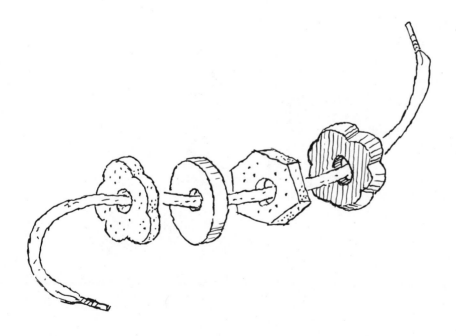

Level IV

Objective 4: Identifies primary colors (red, yellow, blue)

Materials
>Three toy helicopters in primary colors
>Three toy balloons in primary colors
>Three marbles in primary colors
>Three toy harmonicas in primary colors

Activity
>This activity can be used to learn classification skills as well as the primary colors. The child may be asked to group the toys by toy category as well as by color. The teacher then asks the child to name items of each primary color.

Group Size
>Individual
>Small group

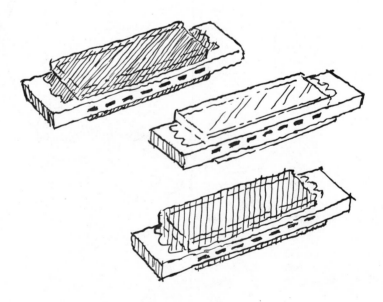

Objective 4: Identifies primary colors (red, yellow, blue)

Materials
> Three small baskets in primary colors
> Three miniature doll hangers in primary colors

Activity
> The teacher first names the colors of the baskets and hangers. Next the teacher may ask the child to point to a red basket, a blue hanger, and so forth. As a more difficult task, the child can be asked to put a yellow hanger in a blue basket and so on.

Group Size
> Individual
> Small group

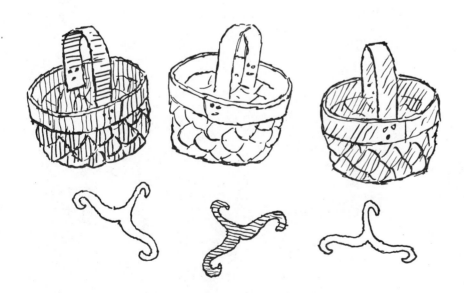

IDENTIFICATION, DISCRIMINATION, AND CLASSIFICATION SKILLS

Level IV

Objective 5: Identifies likenesses and differences in two or
more objects (shape, size, color)

Materials
Coke bottle caps
7Up bottle caps
Pepsi bottle caps

Activity
The teacher presents the array of bottle caps to the child and discusses
with him or her the likenesses and differences in the bottle caps. The
teacher then asks the child to place the caps in three groups such that
caps in each group are alike. The child then picks up two bottle caps that
are the same and two that are different. The process can be repeated with
three caps.

Group Size
Individual
Small group
Large group

> Objective 5: Identifies likenesses and differences in two or
> more objects (shape, size, color)

Materials
> A string clothesline with strips of green, yellow, and orange paper
> attached
> Green, yellow, and orange clothespins

Activity
> The teacher leads a discussion of how the clothespins are alike and differ-
> ent. After the discussion the children are asked to attach the clothespins to
> the clothesline by matching them to the correct colored strip of paper.

Group Size
> Individual
> Small group

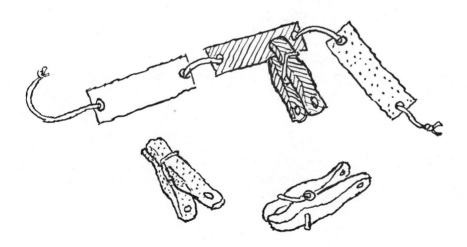

Level IV

Objective 5: Identifies likenesses and differences in two or
more objects (shape, size, color)

Materials
Eight pairs of ties cut from posterboard and covered with the same
material. Yarn is attached to each tie so that it may be worn by the
child.

Activity
The teacher leads a discussion of likenesses and differences in the ties.
The child is then invited to put on a tie and find the tie that matches.

Group Size
Small group
Large group

Objective 6c: Discriminates differences (opposites) in:
textures (rough/smooth)

Materials
A large, flat box with one half of the surface covered with sandpaper,
the other half covered with satin or another smooth material
A collection of rough and smooth objects

Activity
The teacher demonstrates the concept of rough and smooth by asking the
child to pick up each object and feel it while the teacher identifies it as
either rough or smooth. The teacher then asks the child to sort out the
objects by placing them on the rough or smooth side of the box.

Group Size
Individual

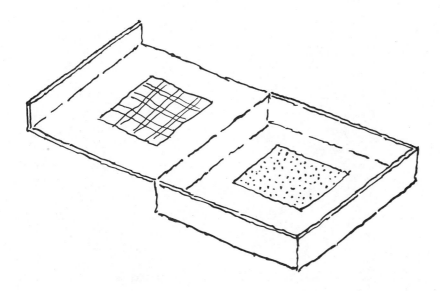

IDENTIFICATION, DISCRIMINATION, AND CLASSIFICATION SKILLS

Level IV

> Objective 7: Identifies spatial relationships: far/near; in/out; front/back, high/low

Materials
>   Small jewelry box
>   Small plastic animal

Activity
>   The teacher will demonstrate position words such as *in, out, far, near*, and so on, by placing the mouse in different positions relative to the box. The teacher then asks the child to place the mouse in different positions as the teacher names each position.

Group Size
>   Individual
>   Small group

> Objective 7: Identifies spatial relationships: far/near; in/out;
> front/back; high/low

Materials
   A birdhouse made from a shoe box
   A small bird mounted on a length of dowel

Activity
   The teacher demonstrates the position words by naming them as the bird
   is put in the various positions in relation to the birdhouse. The teacher
   then asks the child to put the bird in each position as it is named. As a final
   step the teacher places the bird in each position and asks the child to
   name that position.

Group Size
   Individual
   Small group

IDENTIFICATION, DISCRIMINATION, AND CLASSIFICATION SKILLS

Level IV

> Objective 9: Identifies and discriminates actions: run; walk; jump

Materials

A set of different picture cards, each representing a certain action taking place

Activity

The teacher leads a discussion with the child about the action on each picture card. Then the teacher places the cards face down in a stack. The child draws each card and identifies the action pictured.

Group Size

Individual

Small group

Objective 9: Identifies and discriminates actions: run; walk;
jump

Materials
A booklet with photographs of a child demonstrating the different actions

Activity
The teacher discusses with the child the actions depicted in the photographs. The teacher then asks the child to identify the actions as each photograph is shown.

Group Size
Individual
Small group

IDENTIFICATION, DISCRIMINATION, AND CLASSIFICATION SKILLS

Level IV

Objective 10: Classifies objects by more than one property

Materials

A collection of small toys and other objects that have common attributes

Activity

The teacher presents the array of objects and asks the child to use some of the objects to make a group of things that are alike in some way. After the child has classified using one attribute, the teacher asks why the child grouped the objects in that manner. The child returns the objects to the array. Next the teacher asks the child if there is another way to group the objects. Again, the child is asked why the objects were put in that particular group.

Group Size

Individual

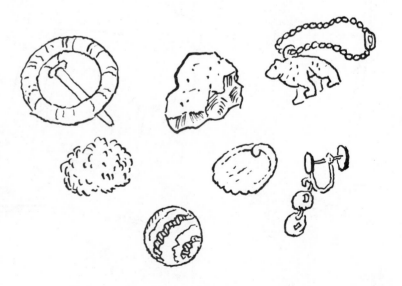

Objective 10: Classifies objects by more than one property

Materials
Marbles of two different sizes and colors

Activity
The teacher asks the child to find two different ways to group the marbles. When the task is completed, the teacher asks how the child decided to group the marbles.

Group Size
Individual

IDENTIFICATION, DISCRIMINATION, AND CLASSIFICATION SKILLS

Level IV

Objective 10: Classifies objects by more than one property

Materials

Small plastic figures of horses, cowboys, and Indians in several colors

Activity

The teacher asks the child to group the figures by an attribute. When the child has finished grouping, the teacher asks why the child grouped the figures as he or she did. Then the teacher asks the child to group the figures again, according to a different attribute.

Group Size

Individual

Small group

Objective 10: Classifies objects by more than one property

Materials

A collection of bottle and jar lids of varying sizes, shapes, types of construction, and so on

Activity

The teacher asks the child to sort the lids into groups. Several different combinations can be made, such as the following:

Lids with and without writing
Lids that screw on and snap on
Lids made of metal and of plastic

Group Size

Individual
Small group

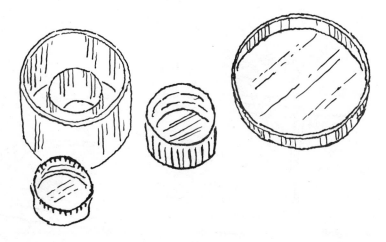

> Objective 12: Classifies by condition: hot/cold; wet/dry;
>   old/new

Materials
> Two pictures featuring hot or cold
> Two pictures featuring wet or dry
> Two pictures featuring old or new

Activity
> The teacher gives the child two pictures at a time featuring a pair of conditions and asks the child to identify which condition is depicted in each picture. The process is repeated with each set of conditions.

Group Size
> Individual
> Small group

Objective 1: Identifies spatial relationships: top/bottom;
              over/under

Materials
   A booklet of snapshots showing a child in the various spatial positions

Activity
   The teacher discusses pictures with the child, naming the positions illustrated in each snapshot. The teacher then asks the child to find the snapshot that illustrates the position word as it is named by the teacher.

Group Size
   Individual
   Small group

Level V

> Objective 5: Identifies colors (green, orange, purple, brown, black, and white)

Materials
> An egg carton with a well painted in each secondary color and black and white
> A collection of small plastic rings usually sold for children to make chains by connecting them

Activity
> The child puts the colored rings in the correct egg wells and names the colors that have been sorted.

Group Size
> Individual

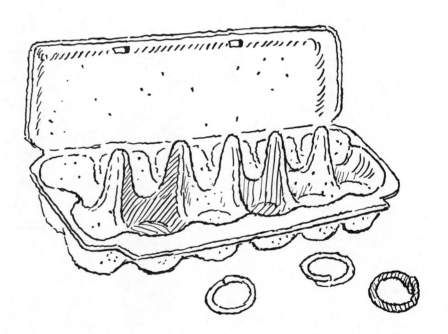

> Objective 5: Identifies colors (green, orange, purple, brown, black, and white)

Materials

Kites cut from construction paper and glued onto cards representing each of the secondary colors. Details are added with a marking pen.

Activity

The teacher presents the kites to the child one at a time and identifies the color. The teacher then names a color and the child points to the kite of that color. As a last step, the teacher holds up a kite and the child names the color.

Group Size

Individual

Small group

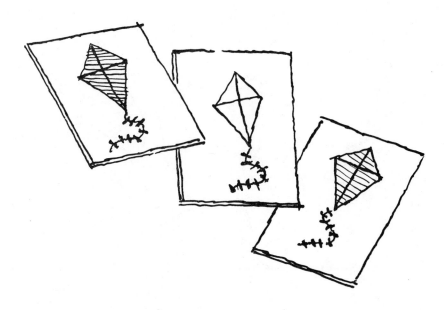

Level V

Objective 5: Identifies colors (green, orange, purple, brown, black, and white)

Materials

Colored picture cards

Activity

This activity assumes the child has knowledge of colors used. After reviewing the colors of the pictures, the teacher makes statements about the pictures. The children must determine if the statement is true or false. Examples of color statements are:

"The boy's shirt is purple."
"The tree is green."

Group Size

Small group
Large group

Objective 7: Classifies colors by intensity (dark/light, darker
than/lighter than)

Materials

Four pens of varying shades of one color

Activity

The child is given time to explore using the pens with paper. Following the
exploration the teacher and child discuss the concepts of dark and light,
darker than and lighter than. The teacher asks the child to arrange the
pens from light to dark. A follow-up activity is to place the pens in random
order and ask the child to find the one that is lighter than the one selected
by the teacher, darker than, and so forth.

Group Size

Individual

Small group

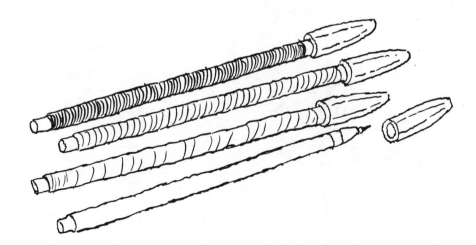

Level V

Objective 8: Classifies foods (fruits, vegetables, meat)

Materials
>   Pictures of fruits, vegetables, and meat cut from magazines and glued
>   to paper plates
>   Three brown shopping bags, each with a picture of fruits, vegetables,
>   or meat

Activity
>   The teacher asks the child to categorize the food pictures by placing them
>   in the appropriate shopping bag.

Group Size
>   Individual
>   Small group

Objective 8: Classifies foods (fruits, vegetables, meat)

Materials

A deck of thirty cards with ten pictures each of meat, fruit, and vegetables.

Activity

The cards are turned over and drawn. After drawing a card, a child identifies the food category of meat, fruit, or vegetable. The child must also be able to name the food item. If the card is identified correctly, the child keeps the card. If the card is not identified correctly, it is returned to the bottom of the deck. Each child takes turns drawing and identifying cards. When all cards have been drawn and identified, the child with the most cards is the winner.

Group Size

Small group

Level V

> Objective 8: Classifies foods (fruits, vegetables, meat)

Materials
> A collection of pictures in the three food categories cut from magazines and mounted on tag board

Activity
> The teacher leads a discussion with the children about what the food categories are and which pictured items belong in each category. The teacher then asks the child to point to a food that is a vegetable, a fruit, a meat, and so on. The last step is for the teacher to point to a food item and ask the child to name it and the category it belongs to.

Group Size
> Individual
> Small group
> Large group

Objective 11: Identifies and classifies common objects by
shape (circle, rectangle, triangle, oval, square)

Materials

Four margarine tubs, each with a round, square, rectangular, or triangular shape glued to its lid

A collection of small objects that are representative of each shape

Activity

The teacher presents the array of objects to the child and demonstrates
the relationship between the object and the shape on each margarine
tub. The teacher then asks the child to sort the objects according to shape
by putting them in the appropriate containers.

Group Size

Individual

Small group

Level V

Objective 11: Identifies and classifies common objects by
shape (circle, rectangle, triangle, oval, square)

Materials

A collection of pictures of common household items that depict the
shapes, which have been cut from magazines or catalogs and
mounted on cardboard. The pictures can be made self-correcting
by drawing the symbol for the correct shape on the back.

A shallow box with representations of two shapes on each side as
shown below

Activity

The child is to look at each picture and place it in the box showing the
correct shape. At the end of the activity the child may turn over the cards
to check for the correct shape symbol.

Group Size

Individual

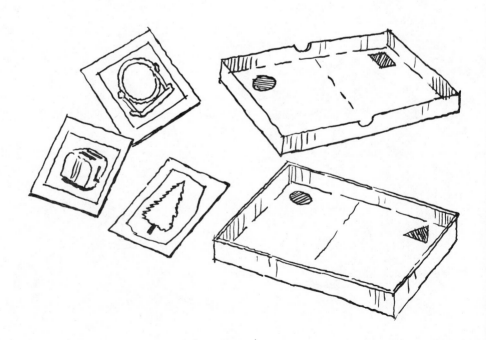

> Objective 11: Classifies common objects by shape (circle, rectangle, triangle, oval, square)

Materials
> Five large cards with a picture of a circle, rectangle, triangle, oval, and
> square
> A collection of picture cards of objects that represent the five figures

Activity
> The pictures of the five shapes are laid on the table and discussed by the
> teacher and child. The teacher then asks the child to match the pictures of
> objects with the correct shape.

Group Size
> Individual
> Small group

Objective 12: Seriates (arranges) objects by size

Materials
> Cardboard tubes cut into different lengths and covered with contact paper

Activity
> The child is given an array of tubes and asked to order them by size from small to large or from large to small.

Group Size
> Individual

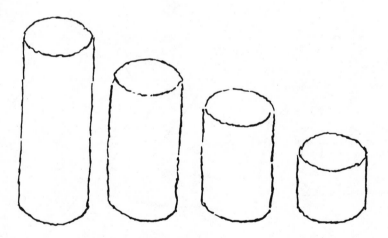

Objective 12: Seriates (arranges) objects by size

Materials
Ten pictures, each with different-sized bird on it. The pictures are glued to strips of posterboard.

Activity
The child is asked to arrange the birds from smallest to largest or from largest to smallest.

Group Size
Individual

Objective 12: Seriates (arranges) objects by size

Materials
Four crocheted squares in ascending sizes

Activity
The teacher asks the child to order the squares. This may be done by lining them up from small to large or from large to small. Another possibility is for the child to order them in a stack with the largest square on the bottom.

Group Size
Individual

Objective 12: Seriates (arranges) objects by size

Materials
    Six cards each with a heart of a different size drawn on it

Activity
    The child is asked to order the hearts from largest to smallest or from smallest to largest.

Group Size
    Individual

SUMMARY

The preoperational child aged from two to seven years moves through one of the most significant periods of human development. Two major aspects of it are the development of concepts and the development of language.

Essential to cognitive development is the ability to think. In order to add to his or her knowledge, the child must be able to use thought to organize information and solve problems. During the preoperational period the child's understanding of thought begins with the inability to understand that mental processes are separate from physical behaviors. The older child has progressed to the recognition not only that do people use thought processes, but also that each individual has separate thoughts.

The preoperational child learns concepts and language in a complementary fashion through active interaction with the materials and experiences provided in her or his environment. The role of the parent and teacher in the learning process is to provide information and experience that will allow the child to learn through exploration and other forms of active involvement. The checklist and accompanying activities describe characteristics of cognitive development and experiences the teacher can provide in the child's environment that will lead to the acquisition of concepts. As a result of involvement with opportunities to identify or name, discriminate, seriate, and classify, the preoperational child will add to his or her knowledge of the world and how it may be organized.

REFERENCES

Copple, C.; DeLisi, R.; and Sigel, I. "Cognitive Development." In B. Spodek (ed.). *Handbook of Research in Early Childhood Education.* New York: Free Press, 1982.

Hohmann, M.; Banet, B.; and Weikart, D. *Young Children in Action: A Handbook for Preschool Educators.* Ypsilanti, Mich.: High Scope Press, 1979.

Piaget, J. *The Child's Conception of the World.* New York: Harcourt, Brace, 1929.

Piaget, J. *The Origins of Intelligence in Children.* New York: Norton, 1952.

Prutting, C.A. "Process/'pros/'ses/n: The Action of Moving Forward Progressively from One Point to Another on the Way to Completion." *Journal of Speech and Hearing Disorders* 26 (1979): 185–198.

Thibault, J.P., and McKee, J.S. "Practical Parenting with Piaget." *Young Children* 38 (1982): 18–27.

Vygotsky, L.S. *Thought and Language.* Cambridge, Mass.: MIT Press, 1962.

Wellman, H.M. "The Foundations of Knowledge: Concept Development in the Young Child." In S.G. Moore and C.R. Cooper (eds.). *The Young Child Reviews of Research, Volume 3.* Washington, D.C.: National Association for the Education of Young Children, 1982.

CHAPTER 4

Mathematics

Mathematics is another area of concept development that can be partially understood using Piaget's stages of development. The preoperational child, who cannot yet conserve, uses consistent strategies to understand numbers and number relationships. This chapter addresses how children develop concepts in math, discusses the Quantitative and Problem-Solving Checklist, and provides activities for the checklist.

HOW CHILDREN DEVELOP CONCEPTS IN MATH

The concepts and skills in mathematics that children acquire during the early childhood years lay the foundation for later knowledge in arithmetic. Gelman and Gallistel (1978) have divided number knowledge into two distinct types, number extraction and number reasoning. Preoperational children are able to develop skills in both types of mathematics.

In the first category, number extraction, counting and ordering are the skills acquired by the preschool child. Young children often use unconventional methods of counting. Frequently they skip numbers or change the order of numbers as they count. Although the process may be inaccurate at first, Gelman and Gallistel have pointed out that young children do consistently demonstrate important understanding about numbers. First, children as young as two or three years of age know that every item should be counted just once. Second, although the words used for counting may be inaccurate, the child understands that the words are used in a stable sequence. Finally, young children understand that the proper count of an array of items is not dependent on counting in one particular order. The order of counting may change, but the total counted will be consistent.

Counting is fundamental to more complex mathematical concepts. Wang, Resnick, and Boozer (1971) proposed that numerals are easier to learn once the child has learned to count. Older children use the principles of beginning counting to engage in larger counts. Barr (1978) determined that kindergarten children learn to use two-digit numeration more effectively through counting than by grouping sets by tens and ones. Groen and Resnick (1977) taught four and a half year olds to add by counting two small groups of objects followed by counting the combined set.

In the area of number reasoning, young children have skills that allow them to solve numerical problems. Children understand the equality of two sets if they are able to count the numbers of items in the sets. Later children are able to reason about numbers when they cannot achieve a total count.

As in other areas of cognitive development, young children develop concepts about mathematics as they actively seek and interpret their experiences with numbers. Wellman (1982) suggests that young children engage in number-related activities spontaneously. Likewise, Constance Kamii (1982) asserts that the child is his or her own source of knowledge about mathematics; it is not taught through social transmission. Again, how children learn mathematical concepts has implications for the roles of parents and teachers in the learning process.

IMPLICATIONS FOR EDUCATION

Because mathematics instruction in early childhood is closely related to the developmental levels of the child, the urgency for early childhood teachers, including primary teachers, to accept the developmental needs of children is particularly relevant. Because most children in preschool and primary classrooms are functioning at the preoperational level, math experiences in these grades should stress using concrete materials first, followed by giving paper-and-pencil tasks to older children when they have developed an understanding of the concepts. Kamii (1982) cautions against excessive use of workbooks or worksheets, which focus on the production of correct written answers rather than on the child's process of thinking. Kamii reminds us that because the child initiates and elaborates knowledge by reflecting on number relationships derived from personal experiences, the teacher should strive to build on the knowledge the child has already constructed.

The concern for provision of experiences in math that will permit the child to move from the concrete to the abstract and from the simple to the complex in developing mathematical concepts has broader implications. Sheila Swett perceived that the theory could be expanded and applied to teaching the learning disabled. Swett (1978) found that learning-disabled children are weak in language skills. She proposed that understanding math concepts, which use visual and concrete experiences, could assist learning-disabled children to organize their thoughts, which in turn would lead them toward mastery of the more abstract demands of language development.

Relatively recent research in the function of the brain hemispheres also reinforces the importance of using concrete materials in teaching math. McGuinness (1979) reported finding sex differences in early childhood development. Females excel in fine motor control, sequential programming, and verbal abilities, which are associated with the function of the left brain. Males, on the other hand, are superior in gross motor skills, learn about their environment by manipulation and action, and excel in three-dimensional spatial perception, which is related to the functions of the right brain. McGuinness also reported research giving evidence that the attraction of boys to the properties of objects is relevant to their subsequent superiority in higher mathematics. McGuinness supports the idea that schools should rearrange primary classrooms to give boys an opportunity to explore in order to learn about their world. At the same time, girls should experience activities that will enhance their understanding about the properties of the physical world and objects in space.

Grayson Wheatley (1977) has stressed the development of both hemispheres in math in order to develop problem-solving abilities. Wheatley has suggested that our schools reward left-hemisphere activities, which stress sequential tasks, analysis, and language. The right hemisphere, which processes many stimuli at once, perceives holistically, and uses imagery and intuition, is rarely activated. Wheatley has proposed that problem solving, an integral part of mathematics, would improve with greater use of the right hemisphere of the brain. To achieve this, he has advocated that teachers and curriculum writers use tasks that are open ended and require investigation.

Kamii (1982) outlined six principles of teaching that suggest how the teacher can foster the development of logico-mathematical knowledge:

1. The creation of all kinds of relationships. Encourage the child to be alert and to put all kinds of objects, events, and actions into all kinds of relationships.
2. The quantification of objects
    a. Encourage the child to think about number and quantities of objects when these are meaningful to him.
    b. Encourage the child to quantify objects logically and to compare sets (rather than encouraging him to count).
    c. Encourage the child to make sets with movable objects.
3. Social interaction with peers and teachers
    a. Encourage the child to exchange ideas with his peers.
    b. Figure out how the child is thinking, and intervene according to what seems to be going on in his head (p. 27).

USING THE QUANTITATIVE AND PROBLEM-SOLVING CHECKLIST

The checklist incorporates developmental skills, sequential skills, and divergent thinking, all of which leads to problem-solving abilities. As a result, some objectives on the checklist are open ended, indicating that activities in these areas should be provided frequently in the learning environment. Developmental activities based on Piagetian theory can be administered either to determine if a child has achieved the level of development indicated by the task or to provide the child with experiences that meet the stated objective. Some objectives are sequential and may be taught and assessed for mastery.

The Problem-Solving Checklist follows. Following that is an annotated list that explains the checklist objectives and provides activities to match.

FROST WORTHAM DEVELOPMENTAL CHECKLIST

CONCEPT DEVELOPMENT
*PRESCHOOL**
Math: Quantitative and Problem Solving
Color code: Orange

LEVEL III	Introduced	Progress	Mastery
1. Manipulates and experiments with simple machines			
2. Counts by rote from 1 to 5			
3. Forms creative designs with materials			
4. Uses construction materials for multiple purposes			
5. Perceives objects from different visual perspectives			
LEVEL IV			
1. Counts by rote from 1 to 10			
2. Demonstrates the concept of number through 5			
3. Orders the numerals 1 to 5			
4. Understands the concepts of *first* and *last*			
5. Identifies:			
a) penny			
b) nickel			
c) dime			
6. Compares differences in dimension (taller/shorter, longer/shorter, thinner/wider)			
7. Demonstrates one-to-one correspondence			

**FROST WORTHAM DEVELOPMENTAL
CHECKLIST (continued)**

LEVEL V

	Introduced	Progress	Mastery
1. Counts by rote from 1 to 50			
2. Demonstrates the concept of number through 10			
3. Orders the numerals 1 to 10			
4. Writes numerals for sets 1 to 10			
5. Identifies pairs of familiar objects (shoes, socks, gloves, earrings)			
6. Groups objects into sets of equal number			
7. Compares elements of unequal sets (more than/fewer than)			
8. Combines (adds) the total number in two small groups			
9. Uses ordinal concepts up through *third*			
10. Identifies:			
a) penny			
b) nickel			
c) dime			
d) quarter			
11. Compares distance (height, width) to an independent object			
12. Compares volumes in separate containers			
13. Tells time to the hour			

*Developed by Joe Frost and Sue Wortham; revised and validated, July 1980. Used by permission of Joe L. Frost.

**FROST WORTHAM DEVELOPMENTAL CHECKLIST
QUANTITATIVE AND PROBLEM SOLVING**

LEVEL III

1. *Manipulates and experiments with simple machines*
   This is an exploratory activity, the purpose of which is to give the child experiences in hypothesis testing and creative thinking. Some examples of simple machines are a pencil sharpener and a manual egg beater.
2. *Counts by rote from 1 to 5*
   In this objective the child demonstrates the ability to count verbally to 5. A sense of number is not required, but the child is expected to name correctly the numbers in sequence.
3. *Forms creative designs with materials*
   This is an open-ended activity used to provide opportunities for explo-

ration. Many kinds of expressive materials, including clay and drawing and painting materials, are made available to the children. The teacher uses observation techniques to become aware of the multiplicity of uses that the child makes of the material while exploring the physical properties and expressing ideas.

4. *Uses construction materials for multiple purposes*
    Creative exploration is also the purpose of this objective. The teacher places small and large construction materials, such as unit blocks and table construction games, in the environment on an ongoing basis. The teacher observes the change and development in the child as the child uses the materials over a period of time.

5. *Perceives objects from different visual perspectives*
    The purpose of this Piagetian task is to determine whether the child is

egocentric, that is, dominated by his or her own point of view. Specifically, the task determines whether the child can describe or account for a physical situation as if seen from a position that is different from his or her own. To assess this ability, the teacher places a three-dimensional scene on a low table and asks the child to study it from several sides. The teacher then asks the child to describe how the setting would look from a different side of the table than the side the child is facing. Although able to see the entire setting, the child must be able to mentally place herself or himself in another position in relationship to the setting.

LEVEL IV

1. *Counts by rote from 1 to 10*
    The child is able to name the numbers in correct order from 1 to 10. A sense of number is not necessary, just the ability to count correctly.

2. *Demonstrates the concept of number through 5*
    The child is able to match the number of items with the correct numeral. These should be presented in and out of sequence to determine the child's mastery. The teacher may present a number of items and ask the child to select the numeral to match or may reverse the process by presenting the numeral and asking the child to select the appropriate number of items to match the numeral.

3. *Orders the numerals 1 to 5*
    The child is able to sequence numerals physically and to identify the numerals and order them sequentially. To assess the child's ability, the teacher may present the numerals in mixed order and ask the child to place them in the correct order.

4. *Understands the concepts of* first *and* last
    This is the first level of comprehending ordinal numbers. The child understands that *first* relates to the numeral 1 and *last* is any final element in a series. The concept can be assessed by having several children stand in a line and asking the child being assessed to identify which person is first and which is last. As an alternative, the teacher may place small figures such as dogs in a line and ask the child to pick up the first dog and the last dog.

5. *Identifies: penny; nickel; dime*
    Given an array of three kinds of coins, the child can pick up each coin as it is named by the teacher. At a more difficult level the teacher picks up the coin and asks the child to name it.

6. *Compares differences in dimension (taller/shorter, longer/shorter, thinner/ wider)*
    The child is learning dimensional concepts such as *tall*, *short*, *thin*, and *wide*. When shown an array of items of different dimensions using height or width, the child identifies which is taller and shorter or which

is thinner and wider. At first the child is asked to compare only two items; later more items can be added.

7.   *Demonstrates one-to-one correspondence*

This is also a Piagetian task. The child is able to determine that two sets are equivalent by matching, one by one, items of the second set with items of the first set. The child who can *conserve* knows that the two sets are equivalent, regardless of the arrangement of items within the two sets. To assess the task, the teacher first arranges the two sets of items in a parallel fashion and asks the child if both sets are the same. After the child has determined equivalency, the teacher spreads out the items in the second set and repeats the question. The child is permitted to reconstruct the second set using one-to-one correspondence to reaffirm equivalence of the two sets.

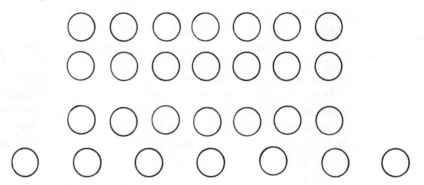

LEVEL V

1.   *Counts by rote from 1 to 50*

This objective is the same as objectives 2 and 1, from Levels III and IV, respectively, but requires the child to be able to name the numbers in correct order as far as 50.

2.   *Demonstrates the concept of numbers through 10*

The child is able to match the numeral with the correct number of items. As in Level IV the child can match the numeral to sets of items or construct the sets to match the numerals.

3.   *Orders the numerals 1 to 10*

The child is able to place numerals in correct sequential order. To assess the skill, the teacher gives the child a set of ten numeral cards in mixed order and asks the child to order them.

4.   *Writes numerals for sets 1 to 10*

This objective is more complex than objectives 2 and 3. The child must not only understand the numbers 1 to 10 and be able to identify which numeral goes with each number, but must also be able to write the numeral. Given sets of objects, the child can write the correct numeral to match the set.

5. *Identifies pairs of familiar objects (shoes, socks, gloves, earrings)*
    The concept to be developed is that some items require two to make a
    complete set and that this type of set is called a pair. Some items that
    are arranged in combinations of two are pairs, while others are not.
    The children need many experiences in determining what a pair is and
    what it is not. A collection of real items such as shoes and socks can be
    used to develop this understanding. To assess the skill, the teacher can
    present an array of items containing two of each object, some of which
    form pairs and others that are not thought of as making pairs. The child
    is asked to identify which items in the array are pairs.
6. *Groups objects into sets of equal number*
    This objective, along with objectives 7 and 8 below, prepares the child
    for simple addition. The child begins to use the term *set* and the process
    of working with sets. An additional purpose is for the child to master
    the concept of *equal*. The teacher constructs a set and asks the child to
    construct a second set that is equal to, or the same in number as, the
    first. Each set may be counted to affirm that they are equal.
7. *Compares elements of unequal sets (more than/fewer than)*
    The concept of *equal* in objective 6 is expanded to include *not equal* and
    not the same. To develop the concept of *unequal*, the teacher first
    presents sets that are different in number. After the child has decided
    that the sets are not equal, or unequal, he or she then determines
    which set has more items. Subsequently, the concepts *more* and *fewer*
    are learned through comparing unequal sets. To assess the ability to
    use *more than* and *fewer than*, the teacher presents two unequal sets and
    asks the child to identify the set which has more. Using two different
    sets, the teacher asks the child to identify the set which has fewer
    items. Research has determined that children are able to understand
    the concept *more* before understanding *fewer*.
8. *Combines (adds) the total number in two small groups*
    In this objective the child learns that two sets may be put together to
    form a larger set. The child can count the number of items in each small
    set and compare these sums to the total in the larger set to be sure that
    the two small sets are equal to the larger set. When the child under-
    stands the concept, the teacher can introduce notation by using nu-
    merals to represent the small sets and the larger set. The symbols "+"
    and "=" can be added after this concept is understood.
        To assess the objective, the teacher may ask the child to make a
    large set with the same number of items as in the two small sets that
    have been presented.
9. *Uses ordinal concepts up through* third
    The child learns to make the correlation between cardinal and ordinal
    numbers. In a series of objects, the child is able to make the connection
    between *one* and *first, two* and *second*, and *three* and *third*. To assess the
    skill, the teacher asks the child to identify which in a series of objects is

second, which first, and which third. The teacher can also point to an item in the series and ask the child to indicate whether it is first, second, or third.

10. *Identifies: penny; nickel; dime; quarter*
As in Level IV the child develops the ability to identify and name each denomination of coin. The quarter has been added at this level.

11. *Compares distance (height, width) to an independent object*
This is a Piagetian task to determine if the child can conserve a dimension. The object is for the child to compare the height or width of two objects that are in close proximity. The child determines equivalence of length by using a string or stick to compare the two. In this task the child is also able to use rods of various lengths to form the equivalent of a given rod. The child can determine if the two are equal or if one is longer than the other. The child uses a string or stick to affirm equivalency.

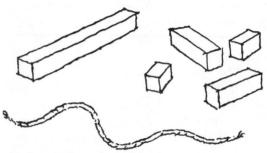

12. *Compares volumes in separate containers*
This is another Piagetian task to assess the child's ability to conserve volume. Two kinds of volume that are commonly compared are water and clay. To determine if the child can conserve volume using water, the teacher first pours water in two identical containers and asks the child if each container is the same. Then the teacher pours water from one container into a third container that has a different dimension and repeats the question. The child can conserve if he or she understands that the amount of water remains the same regardless of the shape of the container.

For the conservation task using clay the teacher begins with two balls of clay that are the same in size and shape. After the child has determined the two balls to be the same, the teacher rolls one into a "sausage" or "snake" and asks the child if the two shapes are still the same or if one is now bigger.

13. *Tells time to the hour*
     The child is able to tell the time when shown a clock face set at different hours.

QUANTITATIVE AND PROBLEM-SOLVING ACTIVITIES

The following activities are based on the premise that the young child must be actively involved in numerical experiences with concrete materials in order to develop mathematical concepts. Experiences are provided for both number extraction (counting) and number reasoning (problem solving). They may be used for teacher-guided experiences or for child-directed episodes. They may also be used for assessment purposes.

Level III

Objective 1: Manipulates and experiments with simple machines

---

Materials
Clamp
Two pieces of scrap wood

Activity
The teacher shows the tool to the child, demonstrates its usage, and then allows exploration.

Group Size
Individual
Two children working together

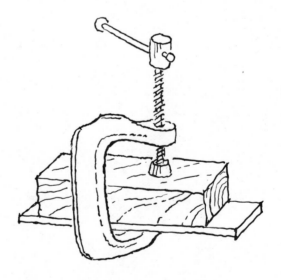

Objective 2: Counts by rote from 1 to 5

Materials
Five buttons

Activity
The teacher places the buttons on a flat surface and demonstrates for the child, counting by rote from 1 to 5. Then the teacher asks the child to count by rote.

Group Size
Individual
Small group

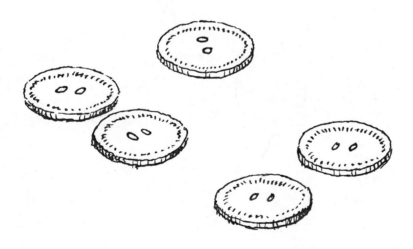

MATH: QUANTITATIVE AND PROBLEM SOLVING

Level III

Objective 2: Counts by rote from 1 to 5

Materials
Five plastic balls

Activity
The teacher lines up the balls and touches each ball while counting by rote from 1 to 5. Then the teacher asks the child to count from 1 to 5.

Group Size
Individual
Small group

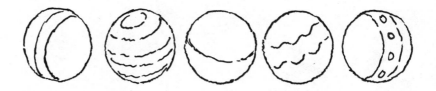

Objective 3: Forms creative designs with materials

Materials
Four shape templates
Blank paper
Colored pencils or crayons

Activity
The teacher shows the child how to trace around the templates. The teacher then demonstrates how the shapes can be turned into new forms by placing them in different positions one on top of the other, using the same shape over again or different shapes. The child is then allowed to experiment using the materials.

Group Size
Individual
Small group

Level IV

Objective 1: Counts by rote from 1 to 10

Materials
>   Ten plastic straws

Activity
>   The purpose of this activity is to help children count by rote. The teacher demonstrates by placing the straws in a row one at a time while counting. The child is then asked to count using the same process.

Group Size
>   Individual
>   Small group
>   Large group

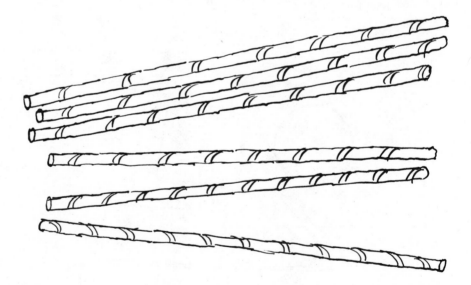

Objective 2: Demonstrates the concept of number through 5

Materials
Five sandpaper numerals glued onto cardboard
Fifteen small coins or counters

Activity
The teacher places the number cards in sequential order and demonstrates for the child how to place the correct number of coins under each card. The teacher then asks the child to repeat the activity. As a more difficult task, the teacher places the cards in random order and asks the child to place the correct number of coins under each card.

Group Size
Individual
Small group

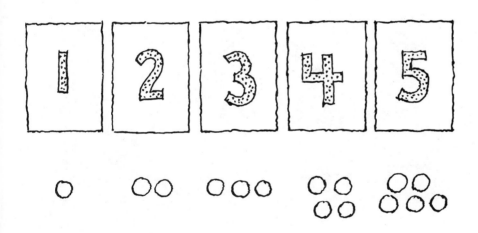

Level IV

Objective 2: Demonstrates the concept of number through 5

Materials

Envelopes with the numerals 1 through 5 on the front
Fifteen small cards with cartoon figures

Activity

The teacher demonstrates for the child the concept of the numbers 1 to 5 using the cards and envelopes with numbers. The teacher then asks the child to put the correct number of picture cards in each envelope.

Group Size

Individual
Small group

Objective 2: Demonstrates the concept of number through 5

Materials
Six Tupperware popsicle molds with the numerals 1 to 5 on five of the
molds
Fifteen popsicle sticks placed in sixth mold

Activity
The teacher demonstrates for the child that each mold should be filled
with the number of sticks that correlates with the numeral on the front of
the mold. The teacher then asks the child to place the correct number of
sticks in each mold.

Group Size
Individual

Level IV

Objective 2: Demonstrates the concept of number through 5

Materials
> Five small plastic boxes of different colors: blue, orange, yellow, pink and green
> Fifteen buttons: one blue, two orange, three yellow, four pink, and five green

Activity
> The teacher presents the array of boxes and buttons. The child is asked to place the buttons in the matching colored container. Then the teacher asks the child to identify which box has one button, which has two buttons, and so forth. Finally, the teacher asks the child to order the boxes from 1 to 5 according to how many buttons are inside.

Group Size
> Individual
> Small group

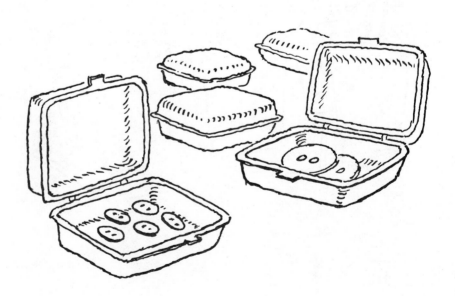

Objective 2: Demonstrates the concept of number through 5

Materials
Posterboard
White and red felt
Envelope

The posterboard is decorated with a picture of an ice cream shop and below it five sundae dishes. Under each sundae dish is written one number from 1 to 5. Five white whipped creams and fifteen red cherries for the sundaes are cut from felt. The cherries are stored in the envelope glued to the back of the posterboard.

Activity
The teacher takes the felt cherries out of the envelope and asks the student to place the number of cherries on the whipped cream of each sundae to match the number written below the ice cream dish.

Group Size
Large group
Small group

Level IV

Objective 3: Orders the numerals 1 to 5

Materials
Large plastic paper clips numbered 1 through 5

Activity
The children arrange the paper clips in proper numerical order on request by the teacher.

Group Size
Individual
Small group

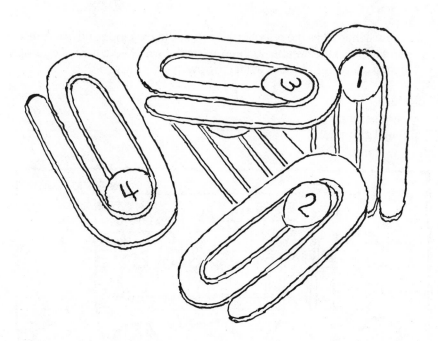

Objective 3: Orders the numerals 1 to 5

Materials

Five small sponges, each marked with a numeral from 1 to 5
Five different hand soaps, each marked with a numeral from 1 to 5

Activity

The student is asked to arrange the sponges in numerical sequence. Next the student visually matches numerals by placing the hand soaps on the corresponding sponges.

Group Size

Individual
Small group

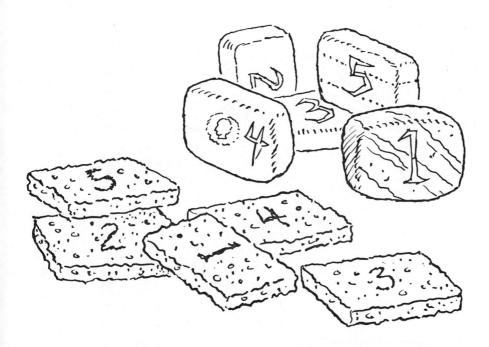

Level IV

Objective 3: Orders the numerals 1 to 5

Materials
>A set of small plastic numerals 1 through 5

Activity
>The teacher presents the numerals in mixed order and demonstrates how to put them in the correct sequence. The teacher again mixes the numerals and asks the child to put them in order.

Group Size
>Individual
>Small group

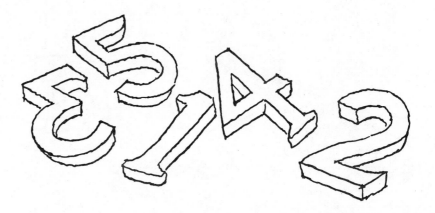

Objective 4: Understands the concepts *first* and *last*

Materials
A cardboard train consisting of an engine, caboose, and several cars
Magnetic strips attached to the back of each piece of cardboard
A metal surface such as a magnetic board, file cabinet, or TV tray

Activity
The teacher asks the child to put the train in order. The child must demonstrate that the engine comes first and the caboose comes last; the order of the other cars does not matter. After the child has arranged the cars, the teacher asks which car is first and which is last. The child may point or verbally identify first and last.

Group Size
Individual
Small group

Level IV

Objective 4: Understands the concept *first* and *last*

Materials
Various lids

Activity
The teacher arranges the lids into a line. The child is asked to pick up the first lid in the line and then the last lid in the line. The teacher rearranges the lids and repeats the procedure.

Group Size
Individual
Small group

Objective 5: Identifies: penny; nickel; dime

Materials
One penny, one nickel, and one dime
Paper and crayons

Activity
The teacher asks the child to point to each coin as it is named. The teacher then points to the coin and asks the chld to name it. As a reinforcing activity, the teacher gives the child paper and crayons to make rubbings of the coins.

Group Size
Individual
Small group

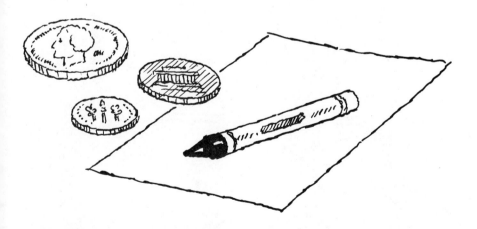

Level IV

Objective 6: Compares differences in dimension (taller/shorter, longer/shorter, thinner/wider)

Materials
Wooden dowels of different diameters and lengths

Activity
The teacher presents the array of dowels and asks the child to select two. The child is asked to compare length and width of the selected dowels. Later the child can compare three or more dowels at a time.

Group Size
Individual
Small group

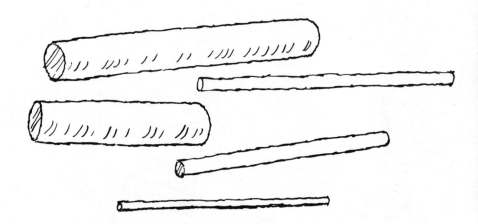

Objective 6: Compares differences in dimension (taller/shorter, longer/shorter, thinner/wider)

Materials
Primary pencils and regular pencils sharpened to various lengths

Activity
The teacher selects a pencil from the array and asks the child to find another pencil that is shorter, taller, thinner, and so forth. The activity continues with another selected pencil of different dimensions.

Group Size
Individual
Small group

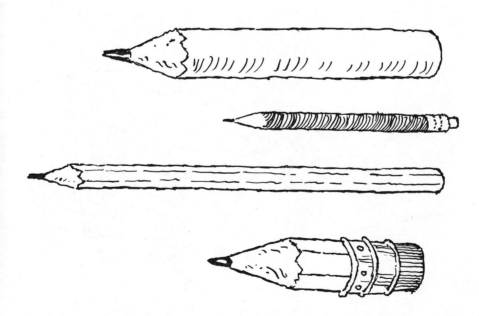

Level IV

Objective 6: Compares differences in dimension (taller/shorter, longer/shorter, thinner/wider)

Materials
Four index cards, each with a picture of a family member

Activity
The teacher presents the cards to the child. First the child compares the height of the various family members. Then the child is asked to order the pictures of the family from shortest to tallest.

Group Size
Individual
Small group

Objective 6: Compares differences in dimension (taller/shorter, longer/shorter, thinner/wider)

Materials
Strips of cardboard cut to different lengths and widths

Activity
The teacher demonstrates for the child the differences in length and width among the various strips. Then the teacher asks the child to select two strips and determine which is taller (or longer) and which is shorter, which is thinner and which is wider, and so forth.

Group Size
Individual
Small group

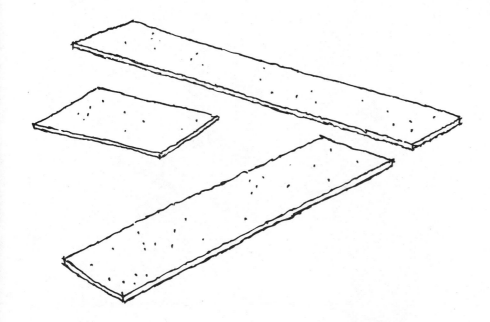

Level IV

Objective 6: Compares differences in dimension (taller/shorter, longer/shorter, thinner/wider)

Materials
A set of six screws of different widths and lengths

Activity
The teacher asks the child to select two screws and compare them by width and length. The child should determine which is taller (or longer) and which is shorter; which is thinner and which is wider.

Group Size
Individual
Small group

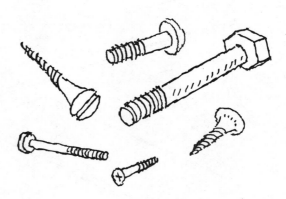

Objective 6: Compares differences in dimension (taller/shorter, longer/shorter, thinner/wider)

Materials
Different lengths of yarn

Activity
The teacher asks the child to place two pieces of yarn side by side to compare their lengths. The child is then asked to identify which piece is longer and which shorter. Later additional lengths may be added.

Group Size
Individual
Small group

MATH: QUANTITATIVE AND PROBLEM SOLVING

Level IV

Objective 7: Demonstrates one-to-one correspondence

Materials
> Five toothbrushes
> Five toothbrush cases

Activity
> The child demonstrates one-to-one correspondence by placing a tooth-brush in each case.

Group Size
> Individual
> Small group

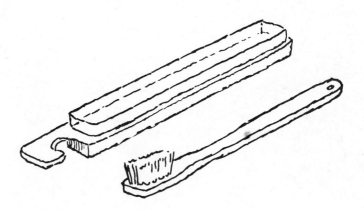

Objective 7: Demonstrates one-to-one correspondence

Materials
> Ten flowers cut from gift wrapping paper mounted on tagboard and
> attached to green pipe-cleaner stems
> Ten miniature fabric bumblebees purchased from a craft shop

Activity
> The teacher demonstrates how to achieve one-to-one correspondence by
> lining up the flowers in a row and matching a bumblebee with each flower.
> The child repeats the process.

Group Size
> Individual
> Small group

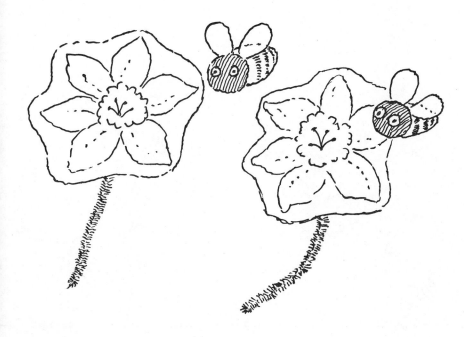

Objective 7: Demonstrates one-to-one correspondence

Materials

Matched sets of black and white plastic horses

Activity

The two sets of horses are placed in rows in one-to-one correspondence. The teacher demonstrates for the child that there is one black horse for each white horse. Using sets of different number the child forms a set of black horses to match the set of white horses to form a one-to-one correspondence between the two sets.

Group Size

Individual

Small group

Objective 7: Demonstrates one-to-one correspondence

Materials
 Ten plastic drinking straws
 Ten paper cups

Activity
 The teacher places the paper cups in a row. The student then determines
 if there are the same number of straws as cups by placing a straw in each
 cup.

Group Size
 Individual
 Small group

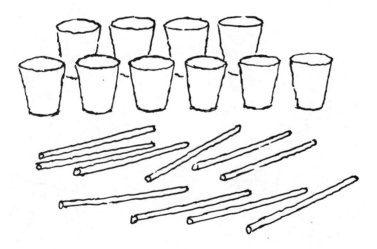

Objective 7: Demonstrates one-to-one correspondence

Materials
> A set of cookie cutters
> A large manila folder with the outlines of the cookie cutter shapes
> drawn on the inside

Activity
> The student matches the cookie cutters with the outlines on the folder to
> determine if there is a cookie cutter for each outline.

Group Size
> Individual
> Small group

Objective 1: Counts to 50

Materials
> Several bags of beans, each with a different number. One bag should contain fifty beans.

Activity
> The teacher shows the bags to the children and asks them questions:
>
> Which bag has the most beans?
> Which bag has the fewest beans?
> How many beans are in each bag?
>
> Each student counts out loud the number of beans in her or his bag. The activity can be repeated after the children have exchanged bags.

Group Size
> Small group

Level V

Objective 2: Demonstrates the concept of number through 10

Materials
> An egg carton with egg wells numbered from 1 to 10
> Dominoes with dots totaling 1 to 10

Activity
> The teacher places the dominoes in a mixed array. The children are asked to count the dots on each domino and then place the domino in the egg well with the appropriate numeral.

Group Size
> Individual
> Small group

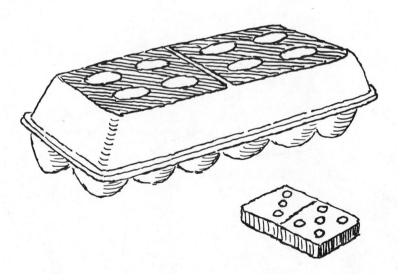

Objective 2: Demonstrates the concept of number through 10

Materials

Large cards with the numerals from 1 to 10 on them

Picture cards of sets containing different numbers of objects

Activity

The teacher places the cards containing numerals in one pile and the cards containing sets in another. The teacher then asks the child to match the numeral cards with the set cards. An optional activity is for the child to order the numeral cards from 1 to 10 and place the appropriate set cards under the numeral cards.

Group Size

Individual

Small group

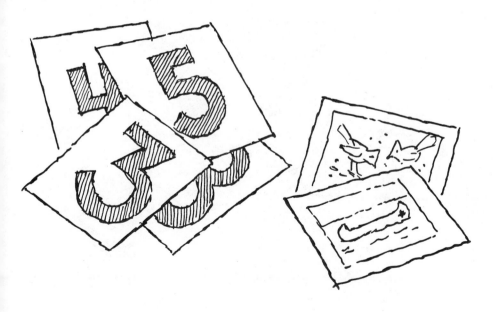

Level V

Objective 2: Demonstrates the concept of number through 10

Materials

A spinner card with numerals 1 through 10

Two game boards with numerals from 1 through 10. There is a slit below each numeral

Ten sets of cards with dots numbered from 1 to 10. Each set is a different color

Activity

Two children can play. The players take turns spinning. The player finds the card of dots that corresponds to the numeral where the spinner stopped. If the spinner lands on a number that is already occupied, the player forefeits a turn. The first player to fill all his or her slots wins.

Group Size

Two children

Objective 3: Orders numerals 1 to 10

Materials
Ten clothespins with numerals from 1 to 10 on them
A small coffee can

Activity
The child empties the can of clothespins onto the desk and then clips the clothespins in correct order on the top of the can.

Group Size
Individual
Small group

Level V

Objective 3: Orders the numerals 1 to 10

Materials
   Numeral cards from 1 to 10

Activity
   The teacher places the cards in random order numeral side up and demonstrates how to order them from 1 to 10. The child is then asked to repeat the activity.

Group Size
   Individual
   Small group

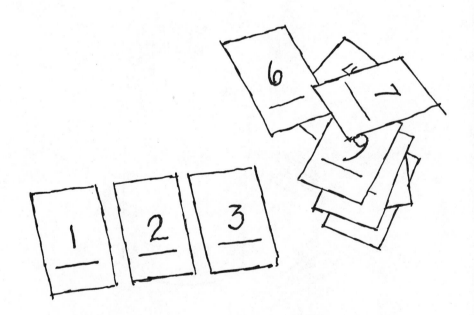

Objective 4: Writes numerals for sets 1 to 10

Materials
A small blank photo album. On each page of the album place various
numbers of toothpicks ranging in number from one to ten.
A wax crayon
A paper towel

Activity
The teacher asks the child to take the crayon and write in the numeral that
corresponds to the number of toothpicks on the album page. When the
activity is completed, the crayon may be wiped off with the paper towel.

Group Size
Individual
Small group

Level V

Objective 5: Identifies pairs of familiar objects (shoes, socks, gloves, earrings)

Materials
Several pairs of large earrings

Activity
The teacher explains to the child what makes a pair of items and demonstrates by arranging the earrings in pairs. The teacher then groups the earrings randomly and asks the child to make appropriate pairs.

Group Size
Individual
Small group

Objective 5: Identifies pairs of familiar objects (shoes, socks, gloves, earrings)

Materials

The teacher cuts out or draws pictures of pairs of objects on paper and glues them to cards. The teacher then cuts the cards into puzzles by using a zigzag design down the center. Each set must be unique (have a different picture and a different cut pattern).

Activity

The teacher discusses the concept of *pair* with the child and demonstrates how to combine the puzzle pieces to make pairs. The child then combines all of the pieces into pairs.

Group Size

Individual

Small group

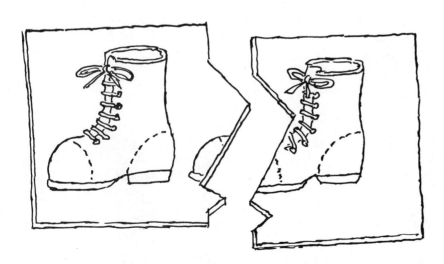

Level V

Objective 6: Groups objects into sets of equal number

Materials

Three sets of objects, each having at least five items

Activity

The teacher demonstrates how to form sets equal in number by making a set with one kind of object and making a second set with an equal number of objects. The teacher then makes a second set with a different number of objects and asks the child to make a second set with a number equal to the teacher's set. The process can be repeated many times using different numbers in sets.

Group Size

Individual

Small group

Objective 6: Groups objects into sets of equal number

Materials
A collection of small plastic Indians
A collection of colored plastic paper clips

Activity
The teacher constructs a set using the paper clips. The child is asked to construct a second set containing the same number of Indians.

Group Size
Individual
Small group

Level V

> Objective 7: Compares elements of unequal sets (more than/fewer than)

Materials
> Two sets of different kinds of nuts (pecans and walnuts)

Activity
> The teacher makes a set from each of the two kinds of nuts. The child counts each set to determine which one has more and which has fewer.

Group Size
> Individual
> Small group

Objective 7: Compares elements of unequal sets (more than/fewer than)

Materials
Matched sets of toy dinosaurs in two colors

Activity
The teacher demonstrates for the child the concepts of equal sets and unequal sets using the dinosaurs. After enough sets have been compared for the child to have a grasp of the concepts *more than* and *fewer than*, the teacher asks the child to compare unequal sets and determine which has more and which has fewer.

Group Size
Individual
Small group

MATH: QUANTITATIVE AND PROBLEM SOLVING

Level V

Objective 7: Compares elements of unequal sets (more than/fewer than)

Materials

Six plastic knives
Five plastic forks
Two plastic spoons

Activity

The teacher first presents two sets that are different in number and the child determines which set has more items in it than the other. The teacher now uses a different combination of two sets and asks the child to select the set with the fewer items. The activity can be repeated.

Group Size

Individual
Small group

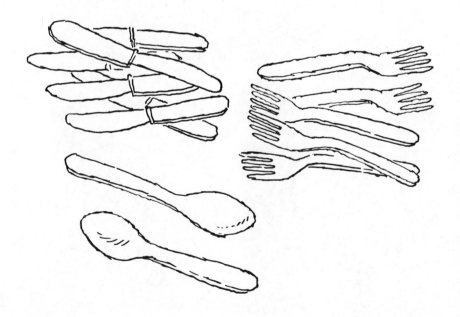

Objective 8: Combines (adds) the total number in two small
groups

Materials
Two dice with numerals 1 through 6
Twelve black and red discs or checker pieces

Activity
The child rolls one die and then forms a pile of discs that match in number
the numeral appearing on top of the die. The child rolls the second die
and forms the second set of discs in the same way. The two resulting sets
of discs are combined to make a larger set. The child then counts the
larger set to determine the total number of discs.

Group Size
Individual
Small group

Level V

Objective 8: Combines (adds) the total number in two small
groups

Materials
A collection of various colors and types of dinosaurs.

Activity
The teacher demonstrates how to combine groups by forming two small
groups of dinosaurs and asks the child how many are in each group. The
teacher then combines the two groups into one and asks the child to
count the dinosaurs in the larger group. The process is repeated using
groups of differing numbers.

Group Size
Individual
Small group

Objective 9: Uses ordinal concepts up through third

Materials
> Three paper cups
> A button

Activity
> The teacher places the four cups on a table and asks the children to close their eyes while a button is hidden under one of the cups. Then the teacher asks the children to open their eyes and guess where the button is, using the terms *first, second*, and *third* to identify the cup they have selected.

Group Size
> Small group

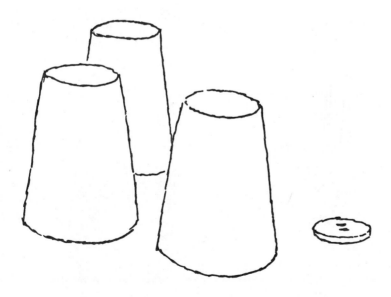

Level V

Objective 12: Compares volumes in separate containers

Materials

Two plastic, disposable cups

One taller glass or jar that will hold the same amount as the plastic cups

Pinto beans, enough to fill the two cups

Activity

By filling both plastic cups, the teacher demonstrates that each can hold an equal amount of beans. Next the beans in one cup are transferred to the tall glass. The teacher asks the child which of the containers now has more beans or if they are the same. This determines whether the child can conserve volume.

Group Size

Individual

Small group

SUMMARY

Although the preoperational child lacks the ability to conserve number and quantity, he or she uses consistent strategies in developing the mathematical concepts that lay the foundation for later learning in arithmetic. The young child learns that in counting, each item should be counted only once and that number words are used in a sequence. Although young children may be inaccurate in counting and in using number words, they do know that items may be counted in any order.

In number reasoning, young children can solve numerical problems if the number of items they are considering is within their ability to count. Because preoperational children need concrete experiences to keep their interest in mathematics spontaneous, parents and teachers should avoid the use of paper-and-pencil activities in favor of opportunities to manipulate objects. Research on brain dominance, sex differences, and the learning disabled supports the use of concrete experiences to meet the needs of children as they organize their understanding of mathematical concepts.

Kamii (1982) supports the theory that as active learners children are able to initiate opportunities that add to their knowledge of number extraction and number reasoning; nevertheless, in six teaching principles Kamii proposes that the teacher also have an active role in encouraging the child to use mathematical concepts and thinking that will foster logico-mathematical knowledge.

REFERENCES

Barr, D. C. "A Comparison of Three Methods of Introducing Two-Digit Numeration." *Journal of Research in Mathematics Education* 9 (1978): 33–43.

Gelman, R., and Gallistel, C. R. *The Child's Understanding of Number.* Cambridge, Mass.: Harvard University Press, 1978.

Groen, G.J., and Resnick, L. B. "Can Preschool Children Invent Addition Algorithms?" *Journal of Educational Psychology* 69 (1977): 645–652.

Kamii, C. "Encouraging Thinking in Mathematics." *Phi Delta Kappan* 64 (1982): 247–251.

Kamii, C. *Number in Preschool and Kindergarten.* Washington, D.C.: National Association for the Education of Young Children, 1982.

McGuinness, D. "How Schools Discriminate Against Boys." *Human Nature* 2 (1979): 82–86.

Swett, S. C. "Math as a Teaching Tool for the Learning Disabled." *Academic Therapy* 14 (1978): 5–13.

Wang, M. C.; Resnick, L. B.; and Boozer, R. F. "The Sequence of Development of Some Early Mathematic Behavior." *Child Development* 42 (1971): 1767–1778.

Wellman, H. M. "The Foundations of Knowledge: Concept Development in the Young Child." In S. G. Moore and C. R. Cooper (eds.). *The Young Child Reviews of Research, Volume 3.* (Washington, D.C.: National Association for the Education of Young Children, 1982.

Wheatley, G. H. "The Brain Hemispheres' Role in Problem Solving." *Arithmetic Teacher* 25 (1977): 36–39.

CHAPTER 5

Oral Language and Reading

Not only do most children learn a language, some learn two or more languages. In this chapter, the process of how children acquire language will be reviewed, followed by an explanation of the Oral Language Checklist and activity worksheets that may be used for assessment or for learning experiences. The second half of the chapter consists of a section on reading readiness and its relationship to oral language, an assessment instrument, and worksheets on activities to use to facilitate reading readiness.

HOW CHILDREN DEVELOP LANGUAGE

By the time the child enters school at age five or six, she or he has acquired the language spoken at home. During the period from birth to six years of age, the child essentially learns the syntax and a substantial part of the vocabulary needed to function in her or his community's language.

The child does not learn language by imitating adults. Courtney Cazden (1972) described imitation as one of the myths about language acquisition. Although children are affected by the language they hear, they form their own rules or syntax for language, which gradually becomes more and more like adult language. Linguists who study children have also proposed that, although children comprehend the adult form of language, they continue to use their own construction (Berko, 1958; Gleason, 1967). For example, a young child usually uses *goed* instead of *went* until the rule for the past tense of irregular verbs is learned. Ursula Bellugi-Klima (1968) gave us an insight on the role that parents play in helping their child with language. Parents do not systematically teach language, nor do they correct misstatements. On the contrary, Ursula Bellugi-Klima found that parents clarify word meanings or correct language that is not socially or factually correct.

Parents talk in a more simple form to the child than they do to other adults; however, as the child's language becomes more complex, so does that of the parent. This simplification of language, called "Motherese" (Newport, 1976), is also used by fathers, nonparents, teachers, and older children when talking to the young child (Garcia, 1982).

There are many variables in language. Each person's language differs in some ways from the language of others. Each individual thus speaks a separate *idiolect*. Groups of people sharing a unique culture or living within a certain geographical area can also share certain language characteristics, called a *dialect*. For example, the black dialect, although different from the dialect of standard English, is a well-developed language. The speech of young children when compared with adult language might also be classified as a dialect.

Because everyone has an idiolect and a dialect, people use different dialects when changing from one language form or level to another, a process called *code switching*. For example, a teacher uses a more formal code when teaching students and switches to less formal language when spending an evening with friends.

Children whose first language is not English thus must learn English as a second language. Heidi Dulay and Marina Burt (1973) determined that second-language acquisition is similar to first-language acquisition. Some significant research has emerged regarding first- and second-language development in bilingual children. Elizabeth Carrow (1971) reported that, although bilingual children score lower than monolingual children on English measures at age three, they do not differ significantly at age six. Huerta (1977) found that children developing two languages have periods when one language forges ahead of the other. Eugene Garcia (1981) found that bilingual children switched languages frequently in their utterances. He proposed that children learning two languages may develop an "interlanguage" in addition to the two separate languages.

IMPLICATIONS FOR EDUCATION

Current research has added new information about how children acquire language; nevertheless, there is much yet to learn. There is also disagreement on how language should be taught once the child reaches educational settings. Although researchers in linguistics are increasingly accurate in describing how the child learns the language spoken in the home before entering school, the role of the teacher in continuing language development in school is not clear. Some feel that the teacher should continue the practices of the mother and encourage language development through talking with the child. Others feel that children, especially those from low-income environments, have specific language needs that require a more formal, structured approach in language instruction. Advocates of the latter support preplanned lessons when the teacher directs language instruction with a group of children. Critics of formal instruction claim that structured language lessons are not based on the child's interests and concerns and therefore may not be relevant to the child. Information about language may not be generalized to the child's language because it may not be compatible with the language structures the child is using at the time.

Some educators support the development of language through extension and expansion. In this role the teacher adds to what the child says or makes a clarifying statement in response to the child's utterance. The teacher also attempts to extend the child's language by increasing the amount the child is able to convert from language that the child simply understands to language that he or she is able to express. Basil Bernstein (1971) designed language training that would improve children's verbal functioning through auditory discrimination, explicit language use, and language structure and vocabulary. Celia Lavatelli (1971) described a similar approach as a "natural" method of language teaching. The teacher serves as a model by producing well-formed sentences the child will hear. The teacher also reinforces the child for using new syntactical forms in activities designed for active involvement in conversations. The teacher's roles to provide models of language and to facilitate awareness of the syntactic structure of language are extremely important if the child's language is to be improved. Frances Schachter and Amy Strage (1982) proposed from their research that there are naturally occurring strategies in talking to young children that have implications for education. They are as follows:

1. Attracting and maintaining the child's attention, as when the adult speaks in a high-pitched voice or addresses questions to the child.
2. Simplifying one's speech with regard to sounds, meanings, grammar and conversational patterns.
3. Repeating and rephrasing one's speech . . .
4. Repeating or rephrasing the child's speech, as when the caregiver expands the child's short utterances.
5. Mapping words onto the child's experiences as when the adult speaks in the present and describes the child's desires or ongoing activities.
6. Speaking for the child, as when caregivers assume the child's role in the conversation, as well as their own role (for instance when they answer their own questions.)
7. Speaking responsively *with* the child, as when caregivers continue the topic of conversation initiated by the child rather than introducing a new topic of their own (p. 90).

USING THE ORAL LANGUAGE CHECKLIST

The checklist for oral language development lists the characteristics of language exhibited by young children in the course of normal language development. On the pages following the checklist, annotations of the objectives describe the meaning of each objective.

In using the checklist teachers should be aware that some checklist objectives refer to the standard dialect of English. Children who use black dialect or who are learning English as a second language may acquire the standard form at a later age than monolingual speakers do. Dialectical or second-language speakers should not be considered different or slow in acquiring language characteristics if this occurs.

An example of a possible conflict between standard and dialectical language is Level V, objective 2, "Uses the correct form of more verbs in informal conversation." William Labov and Paul Cohen (1967) found that speakers of black dialect use the verb differently than it is used in standard English. For example, black-dialect speakers might say, "She be going to the store," rather than, "She is going to the store." The teacher should maintain an awareness that code differences will affect how the checklist is used with children from different backgrounds of language development.

FROST WORTHAM DEVELOPMENTAL CHECKLIST

LANGUAGE DEVELOPMENT*
Oral Language

Color code: Brown

LEVEL III	Introduced	Progress	Mastery
1. Produces language that is mostly intelligible			
2. Recognizes and verbally labels common objects			
3. Responds correctly to simple instructions involving locations in the classroom			
4. Uses sentences of four to five words			
5. Asks questions to gain problem-solving information			
LEVEL IV			
1. Uses simple position words such as *over* and *under*			
2. Uses simple action words such as *run* and *walk*			
3. Uses complete sentences			
4. Uses language for specific purposes (directions, information)			

FROST WORTHAM DEVELOPMENTAL CHECKLIST (continued)

	Introduced	Progress	Mastery
5. Verbalizes routine events ("We're going out to play.")			
6. Averages five-word sentences			
7. Follows simple instructions			
8. Repeats nursery rhymes			

LEVEL V

	Introduced	Progress	Mastery
1. Communicates ideas, feelings, and emotions in well-formed sentences			
2. Uses the correct form of more verbs in informal conversation			
3. Uses the correct prepositions to denote place and position			
4. Uses most personal pronouns correctly			
5. Explains the operation of simple machines			
6. Uses language to get what she or he wants			
7. Can follow instructions containing three parts			

*Developed by Joe Frost and Sue Wortham. Used by permission of Joe L. Frost.

FROST WORTHAM DEVELOPMENTAL CHECKLIST
ORAL LANGUAGE

Oral language development is evaluated by listening to the child talking in informal settings. Because the child has his or her own system for learning to speak, formal language lessons may not indicate whether the child can take a new word or aspect of sentence structure and generalize it to regular usage in speaking. Each of the items on the Oral Language Checklist can be observed in the classroom or outdoor play environment. Following is a brief explanation of each objective for oral language.

LEVEL III

1. *Produces language that is mostly intelligible*
   Although the child mispronounces many words because he or she is still refining how words sound and are produced, most of what the child says can be understood by adults.
2. *Recognizes and verbally labels common objects*
   The child is able to name many of the objects that are familiar in his or her environment, such as table, bed, door, tricycle, and ball.
3. *Responds correctly to simple instructions involving locations in the classroom*

The child is able to follow simple instructions that are given by the teacher, such as "Shut the door," or "Bring me the bottle of glue on my desk."

4. *Uses sentences of four to five words*
When the teacher observes the child using self-initiated language, the sentence length is usually at least four or five words, such as "I want to paint," or "This is the baby's bed."

5. *Asks questions to gain problem-solving information*
The child is able to use questions when help or information is needed. "When can we go outside?" or "How does the fish eat?" are representative of questions that the child at this age might use.

LEVEL IV

1. *Uses simple position words such as* over *and* under
In a conversational context the child uses such words as *over, under, in, on,* or *by* (*beside*) to describe location. Examples are: "Will you sit by me at lunch?" or "My block fell under the chair."

2. *Uses simple action words such as* run *and* walk
During classroom activities the child is able to use action words in sentences, such as "We're not supposed to run," or "He jumped out of the tree."

3. *Uses complete sentences*
The child's syntax has developed to the point of using complete sentences rather than fragments or telegraphic speech. The child says, "Can I have more cookies?" rather than, "More cookies?"

4. *Uses language for specific purposes (directions, information)*
The child is able to use language rather than gestures. The child is able to respond to a question about the location of her or his tricycle by saying, "It's on the porch," rather than pointing to it and saying, "Over there."

5. *Verbalizes routine events ("We're going out to play.")*
When children have acquired enough language, they often talk about things that are happening to them or their environment.

6. *Averages five-word sentences*
Some of the child's utterances are shorter than five words, while others are longer but the average length is about five words. A series of utterances will have to be noted to determine average length.

7. *Follows simple instructions*
This is more complex than Level III, objective 3. The teacher or caregiver gives fewer cues, such as, "Bring me my chair," or "Please hang up your coat."

8. *Repeats nursery rhymes*
As nursery rhymes are learned in classroom activities, the child is able to remember and repeat them.

LEVEL V

1. *Communicates ideas, feelings, and emotions in well-formed sentences*
   The child is able to verbalize feelings that he or she could not express at an earlier period of development. The child might say, "You feel good when your mother hugs you," or "I'm sad when my daddy is gone."
2. *Uses the correct form of more verbs in informal conversation*
   When the child is learning language, many verb forms are used incorrectly as the child tries out forms before settling on the correct one. The child who says, "We went to the movie," rather than, "We goed to the movie," is showing this mastery.
3. *Uses the correct prepositions to denote place and position*
   The child is able to say, "The book is on the shelf," instead of, "It's up there."
4. *Uses most personal pronouns correctly*
   The child is able to use pronouns such as *I* and *me* appropriately. For example, the child says, "I want to go," instead of, "Me want to go."
5. *Explains the operation of simple machines*
   The child is able to verbalize how equipment or objects in the environment function. For example, the child can explain a vacuum cleaner by saying, "The motor makes the air suck up the dirt."
6. *Uses language to get what she or he wants*
   Again, the child is able to verbalize a request rather than use a combination of language and gestures. The child can ask for a blue truck on a shelf by asking, "Can I have the blue truck on that shelf?" instead of pointing and saying, "I want that truck."
7. *Can follow instructions containing three parts*
   The child is able to listen to multiple directions and carry them out. For example, when the teacher says, "Hang up your coat, put your lunch on the shelf, and then you can choose a puzzle to play with," the child is able to remember the instructions and follow them.

ORAL LANGUAGE ACTIVITIES

The activities that follow are correlated to checklist objectives and may be used in several ways. When needed, they can provide an alternative to observation for assessing a child's progress in acquiring a specific element of language. Likewise, they can be used for formal instruction with small or large groups of children. Some activities can be used in a game format or as reinforcement for a language lesson. The activities follow the philosophy that language is acquired through stimulation of the child's natural potential and competence. The teacher's role is to stimulate the acquisition of more sophisticated syntax and vocabulary through informal and structured activities that will facilitate increased competence and performance.

Objective 2: Recognizes and verbally labels common objects

Materials

Common objects such as materials found in the classroom or the home
Sack or "feely bag"

Activity

Place a variety of objects or toys into a bag. In a group the teacher asks the children to individually reach into the bag, pick out an object without looking at it, and name it. After all items have been selected, the activity can be repeated.

This can also be used as a follow-up activity when the children are learning new objects or concepts, such as textures.

Group Size

Small group
Large group

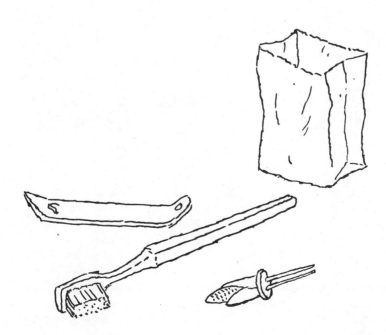

Objective 2: Recognizes and verbally labels common objects

Materials
Plastic animals

Activity
The teacher presents the child with a set of three or four animals such as farm animals or zoo animals. Examples of commonly known zoo animals are elephants, bears, and monkeys. If the child is not familiar with the animals and cannot name them, the teacher first names each animal, then asks the child to show the teacher each animal when asked.

Group Size
Individual
Small group

Objective 2: Recognizes and verbally labels common objects

Materials

A collection of index cards with pictures of common objects found in most homes. The pictures may be cut from catalogs or magazines.

Activity

A small group of pictures is spread on the table. The teacher names the object and the child finds the picture. Another option is for the teacher to select a card and for the child to name the pictured object.

Group Size

Individual
Small group
Large group

Level III

Objective 4: Uses sentences of four to five words

Materials

A collection of pictures of familiar nursery rhymes or stories such as Humpty Dumpty or Little Miss Muffet

Activity

The teacher selects a nursery rhyme or story that has been used with the children many times and is familiar to them. After the teacher presents the picture of a nursery rhyme or story to the child, the child is asked to give a verbal description.

Group Size

Individual
Small group
Large group

Objective 5: Asks questions to gain problem-solving information

Materials
Seven animal cards

Activity
The animals pictured on each card are described by the members of the group. The cards are then placed face down on the table. A child picks a card. The other students in the group ask questions about the characteristics of the animal until the correct animal is identified. The student who correctly identifies the animal selects the next card, and the activity continues.

Group Size
Small group

Level III

Objective 5: Asks questions to gain problem-solving information

---

Materials
　　Two sets each of three or four pictures with common characteristics

Activity
　　Two children are given a set of pictures. The children sit so that they cannot see each other. One child selects a picture to be identified. The other child asks questions about the picture until the correct one is determined.

Group Size
　　Pairs of children

Objective 1: Uses simple position words such as *over* and *under*

Materials

    Cigar boxes with flannel or felt glued to the inside of the lid
    Small felt figures for each box
    A large flannel board with the same figures

Activity

    Each child in the group is given a box with the figures. The teacher asks each child to place the tree on the lid of the flannel board. The teacher can make up a story involving positions of the bird and cat in relationship to the tree. While telling the story, the teacher demonstrates the positions of the cat and bird using the large flannel board. The children follow the teacher's example using their own flannel-board boxes and figures. The children then take turns being the teacher, placing the bird and cat in various positions and saying whether each is over or under the tree, and so forth.

Group Size

    Small group
    Large group

ORAL LANGUAGE

Level IV

Objective 3: Uses complete sentences

Materials

Pictures from magazines, workbooks, and so forth that depict or suggest something is happening. The pictures should be large enough to be easily seen.

Activity

As the teacher shows each picture, the child discusses what is happening, predicts what might be going to happen, or both.

Group Size

Small group

Large group

Objective 4: Uses language for specific purposes (directions, information)

Materials
> Individual flannel boards
> Felt shapes (circles, squares, triangles) in various colors

Activity
> The purpose of this activity is to help children use more explicit language. It can be used with two children or a small group of children.
>
> The children sit so that they cannot see each other's flannel boards. One child makes a picture with his or her shapes. The child then gives instructions for the other children to replicate the picture. When all the children have finished, the children compare their pictures.

Group Size
> Small group

Objective 7: Follows simple instructions

Materials

A felt bulletin board

A clown cut from felt pieces and mounted on the bulletin board as shown below

Felt figures:

flower	umbrella	triangle
hat	balloon	

Activity

As the teacher gives directions to the child, the child selects the appropriate figures and places them on the clown. Examples of directions are:

"Give the clown a blue hat."
"Put a green triangle on the clown's tummy."

Group Size

Small group
Large group

Objective 1: Communicates ideas, feelings, and emotions in
well-formed sentences

Materials

A small box made into a "television set" by cutting out the center for a
screen and attaching a length of paper on dowels with pictures
depicting emotions (see below)

Activity

The teacher gives the children in the group turns at turning the dowels
and describing the pictures on the screen. After the child working the set
has finished describing a picture, the other children in the group are invited to contribute their ideas.

Group Size

Small group
Large group

Level V

Objective 5: Explains the operation of simple machines

Materials
Small hand-operated alarm clock

Activity
After the child has examined and explored the clock, the teacher asks the child to explain the characteristics of the clock and how it works.

Group Size
Individual
Small group

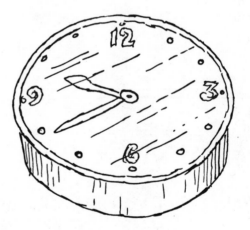

Objective 5: Explains the operation of simple machines

Materials
Mechanical can opener
Compass

Activity
The teacher encourages the child to examine and experiment with the gadget. The teacher then asks the child to describe how the child thinks the gadget works and what it is used for.

Group Size
Individual

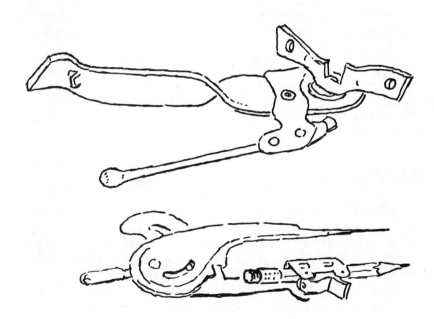

THE RELATIONSHIP BETWEEN ORAL LANGUAGE AND READING

Learning to read is a gradual process. As the child encounters experiences with oral language, literature, and seeing language written down, the relationships between talking and reading develop. Children who are read to and come to school with a large vocabulary find learning to read a fairly easy task. Children who have had limited first-hand experiences with and limited exposure to books may have a difficult time when learning to read.

There is much that the teacher can do to facilitate the reading process with young children. Dorothy Cohen (1966) studied the effects of reading to children. Cohen reported that children who had stories read aloud to them every day gained significantly more in vocabulary and reading achievement than did a control group. John Downing (1970) said that teachers can familiarize children with the function of reading by conducting activities in reading for pleasure, as well as reading for information.

Children's active use of language is also a factor in developing success in reading. Recording the children's accounts of experiences and reading their contributions with them are suggested by many sources. Cullinan, Jaggor, and Strickland (1974) found in their study that children who actively use language in literature activities grow in language ability significantly more than do children who merely hear language. Robinson, Strickland, and Cullinan (1977) express the importance of oral language for reading as follows:

A child's language is the raw material for reading. It contains the meaning the child knows and forms the base for the necessary pairings a child makes between oral and graphic symbols in learning to to read. . . . Most important, for our discussion here, oral language is not only the vehicle but, in another form, printed language is what we teach children to read. The inseparable bonds between the forms of language make it impossible to consider either alone (pp. 22–23).

DETERMINING READINESS FOR READING

When a child should learn to read is a subject of unabated controversy. Much of the argument has centered on whether children should read prior to entering first grade. Advocates of early reading include Dolores Durkin (1968) and Glenn Doman (1963). Others have been strong supporters of teaching children at a later age. In *Better Late Than Early* (1975), Raymond Moore and Dorothy Moore proposed that children are rushed into formal reading instruction much too soon. Waller (1977) suggests that operativity, which is achieved at about seven years of age as described by Piaget, is a partial condition for reading. The child who understands the operations of conservation has achieved operativity.

Also at issue is how to determine if a child is ready to read. Traditionally, readiness has been done through reading readiness inventories based on generally accepted physical and emotional factors, as well as skills thought to be necessary for reading (Guszak, 1972). Another approach to reading readiness is based on Piagetian prerequisites for reading. David Elkind (1974), Eleanor Gibson (1965), John Carroll (1970), and others have worked extensively with Piagetian theory as it relates to reading readiness. Almy, Chittenden, and Miller (1967) studied conservation of number and liquid volume as they correlated with reading achievement. They found in their research that many children are not ready to read before the age of seven, when conservation is acquired. These educators are concerned that many children are given reading instruction before they are developmentally ready to benefit from it.

USING THE READING READINESS CHECKLIST

The checklist is based on the belief that chronological age does not determine readiness to read. The teacher needs to be cognizant of what skills for readiness the child has mastered, as well as where the child is developmentally between the Piagetian stages of preoperations and concrete operations. The checklist provides information on these and other readiness characteristics. Knowing that there is no specific point in time when the child becomes "ready" to read, many indicators are used to determine what kinds of experiences will help the child progress along the continuum into reading. Following are the Reading Readiness Checklist followed by descriptions and examples of checklist objectives, a sample reading readiness instrument, and worksheets of activities. Together these comprise various methods to assess and teach readiness for reading. The teacher may adapt and select portions of the checklist and activities that are compatible with the teacher's philosophy of those factors of readiness that are relevant to early childhood instruction.

FROST WORTHAM DEVELOPMENTAL CHECKLIST

*LANGUAGE DEVELOPMENT**
Reading Readiness

Color code: Yellow

LEVEL V	Introduced	Progress	Mastery
Auditory Discrimination			
1. Discriminates between similar sounds made by different objects			

FROST WORTHAM DEVELOPMENTAL CHECKLIST (continued)

	Introduced	Progress	Mastery
2. Discriminates between initial phonemes (*bat/cat, fat/ rat, plat/flat, sat/hat, fan/Dan*)			
3. Discriminates between medial phonemes (*bet/bit, bat/but, bit/bat, bin/ban, hot/hat*)			
4. Discriminates between final phonemes (*bat/bam, can/cad, bet/bed*)			
Visual Discrimination			
5. Discriminates likenesses and differences in pictured objects, shapes, letters, and words			
6. Uses visual memory to match pictured objects, shapes, letters, and words with one removed			
7. Identifies his or her first name in print			
8. Tracks visually from left to right			
9. Follows left-to-right progression of a pointer while an adult reads			
Letter Knowledge			
10. Matches upper- and lower-case letters			
11. Identifies the letters of the alphabet			
12. Arranges letters in alphabetical order			
13. Matches letters with pictures of objects whose names begin with the same sound as the letter			
Language and Vocabulary			
14. Listens to and follows verbal directions			
15. Identifies the concept of word			
16. Identifies the concept of letter			
17. Invents a story for a picture book			
Oral Comprehension			
18. Locates elements in a picture (tallest, largest, and so forth)			
19. Retells in the correct sequence a story read to him or her			
20. Reorganizes pictures to show the correct story sequence			
21. Answers recall questions about a story			
22. Draws analogies from a story to his or her own experience			
23. Makes value judgments about story events			

FROST WORTHAM DEVELOPMENTAL CHECKLIST (continued)

	Introduced	Progress	Mastery
Experience Chart Skills			
24. Tells experiences for an experience story			
25. Follows left-to-right progression as an adult reads			
26. Identifies recurring words on an experience chart			
27. Suggests titles for experience stories			
Fine Motor			
28. Draws circles with closed ends			
29. Connects dots with straight pencil lines			
30. Copies shapes from a model			
31. Copies alphabet letters from a model			

*Developed by Joe Frost and Sue Wortham. Used by permission of Joe L. Frost.

FROST WORTHAM DEVELOPMENTAL CHECKLIST
READING READINESS

The checklist reflects various approaches to reading readiness. While the traditional readiness skills such as auditory and visual perception are included, equally important are Piagetian tasks of conservation. These are found in the concept development checklist (Identification, Discrimination, and Classification Skills). Emotional and physical development taken from the checklist on socializing (Social Play and Socializing) are also considered. Reading readiness activities on the checklist may be assessed with concrete tasks constructed by the teacher or found in kindergarten kits. A sample informal instrument using pencil and paper activities is also included in the following section. Below is an explanation of each objective on the reading readiness checklist and on the appropriate objectives taken from the concept development and socializing checklists.

LEVEL V
Auditory Discrimination

1. *Discriminates between similar sounds made by different objects*
   The child has developed beyond the point of recognizing gross sounds such as a pencil being tapped or a ringing bell. The child who can discriminate between the sounds of different materials such as sand and rice can differentiate sound boxes like those found in Montessori schools. To make sound boxes, take three empty film cans, aluminum soft drink cans, or other similar containers. Two should contain the

same material, such as sand or rice; the third can should have a different material. Have the child shake the three jars and select the two that produce the same sound.

2. *Discriminates between initial phonemes (bat/cat, fat/rat, plat/flat, sat/hat, fan/Dan)*

   In this skill, as well in objectives 3 and 4, which follow, the teacher is to determine whether the child's auditory ability is fine enough to discriminate between letter sounds. The teacher pronounces each word pair with mouth covered or sits in a position so that the child cannot see the teacher's lips as the words are pronounced. The child repeats the word pairs after the teacher. The teacher listens to the child and determines whether the child has heard and pronounced the letter sounds correctly.

3. *Discriminates between medial phonemes (bet/bit, bat/but, bit/bat, bin/ban, hot/hat)*

   (Same as objective 2.)

4. *Discriminates between final phonemes (bat/bam, can/cad, bet/bed)*

   (Same as objective 2.)

Visual Discrimination

5. *Discriminates likenesses and differences in pictured objects, shapes, letters, and words*

   The students can visually match pictures of objects, shapes, and so on when some are alike and some are different. In a task with concrete materials or in pencil-and-paper tasks, the child can identify which items in a series are alike or can determine which item in a series is different. Following are examples of each.

OBJECT

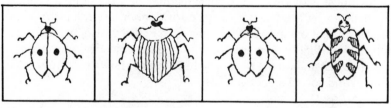

SHAPE

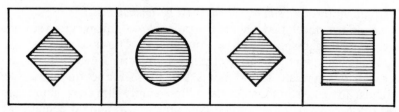

LETTER

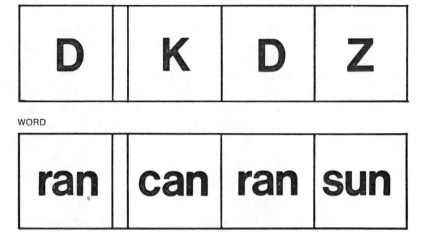

WORD

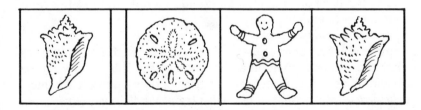

Several examples of likenesses and differences should be included. The tasks should be arranged hierarchically in difficulty.

6. *Uses visual memory to match pictured objects, shapes, letters, and words with one removed*
   In this task the item to be compared is shown to the child and then removed or covered. Without visually comparing, the child completes the task of finding the second item that is similar in the array. This activity is done in the same progression of picture, shape, letter, and word.

   Example: Show the child the first item. Then remove or cover the item and ask the child to select the correct response from the array presented.

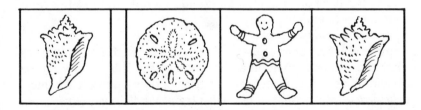

7. *Identifies his or her first name in print*
   The teacher prints three or four names, one of which is the child's. The child identifies the correct name.

Jim   (Kim)
Bob   Sue

8. *Tracks visually from left to right* (Follows moving object with eyes, side to side at reading distance.)
    The teacher takes an object such as a pencil and moves it back and forth at reading distance and asks the child to keep looking as it is moved. During the activity the teacher observes whether the child's eyes are coordinated as they follow the movement of the object.
9. *Follows left-to-right progression of a pointer while an adult reads*
    As an adult reads a story to a child, pointing to the words as they are read, another adult observes to see if the chld is able to follow the left-to-right movement.

Letter Knowledge

10. *Matches upper- and lower-case letters*
    The child is given letters in both upper and lower case and asked to match them. Children usually learn first the letters that are identical in upper and lower case and acquire dissimilar letters later.
11. *Identifies the letters of the alphabet*
    The purpose of this objective is to determine if the child is able to identify letters of the alphabet in random order. A visual array of letters is used. There are several options for letter identification. Depending on the types of experiences the child has had previously, the teacher can determine letter knowledge using upper-case or lower-case letters. Likewise, depending on the teacher's personal preference, identification can be done by letter sounds or letter names. A two-step process is used:
    a.   The teacher names the letters in random order and asks the child to find each letter as it is named.
    b.   The teacher points to letters in random order and has the child name each letter.
12. *Arranges letters in alphabetical order*
    Manipulative letters or an alphabet puzzle can be used. The child takes the letters and places them in alphabetical order. This activity can be done with the entire alphabet at one sitting or only a portion at a time.
13. *Matches letters with pictures of objects that begin with the same sound*
    The student can point to the picture that matches the letter.

Language and Vocabulary

14. *Listens to and follows verbal directions*
     The child is able to process and follow simple directions given in the classroom. Teacher observation of children within ongoing classroom routines can be used to determine this skill.
15. *Identifies the concept of word*
     The student can indicate knowledge of what a word is by drawing a circle around a word in a sentence.

16. *Identifies the concept of letter*
     The student indicates understanding of what a letter is by drawing a circle around a letter in a word.

17. *Invents a story for a picture book*
     A simple picture book is used. The teacher allows the child to examine the pictures and then to tell a story about the book.

Oral Comprehension

The following comprehension skills can be built into storytelling activities or after books have been read to the children.

18. *Locates elements in a picture (tallest, largest, and so forth)*
     Using a picture in a story book or any picture available from a picture file or curriculum kit, the teacher asks children to find different items in the picture.
19. *Retells in the correct sequence a story read to him or her*
     After hearing a story the child is able to tell the main points of the story in the proper order.
20. *Reorganizes pictures to show the correct story sequence*
     Commercial sequence pictures or teacher-made pictures are used for sequencing. Reading readiness workbooks also have sequencing activities that can be cut out and used. The child arranges the pictures in correct order and tells the story.

21. *Answers recall questions about a story*
     After reading or telling a story, the teacher asks the child questions about it that involve memory.
22. *Draws analogies from story to his own experiences*
     After hearing a story the child is able to make relationships between events in the story and experiences in his or her own life.
23. *Makes value judgments about story events*
     After hearing a story the child is able to form an opinion or determine a value such as "right" or "wrong" from his or her own perspective or point of view.

Experience Chart Skills

Reading readiness can also be determined using experience stories dictated by the children. Many of the skills evaluated in isolated activities can also be assessed as part of experience chart activities. The following items are examples of readiness skills determined through experience story activities.

24. *Tells experiences for an experience story*
25. *Follows left-to-right progression as an adult reads*
26. *Identifies recurring words on an experience chart*
27. *Suggests titles for experience stories*

Fine Motor

28. *Draws circles with closed ends*
     The teacher draws a circle on the chalkboard or paper. The child copies the model.
29. *Connects dots with straight pencil lines*
     The teacher makes two lines of dots and models the first line for the child. The child follows the dots from left to right on the second line.
30. *Copies shapes from a model*
         Example:

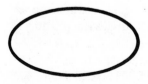

31.　*Copies alphabet letters from a model*
　　　　Example:

Social-Emotional Factors
(From Level V, of Social Play and Socializing Checklist)

1.　*Completes most self-initiated projects*
2.　*Works and plays with limited supervision*
3.　*Engages in cooperative play*
4.　*Listens while peers speak*
5.　*Follows multiple and delayed directions*
6.　*Carries out special responsibilities (for example, feeding animals)*
7.　*Listens and follows the suggestions of adults*
8.　*Enjoys talking with adults*
9.　*Can sustain an attention span for a variety of duties*
10.　*Evaluates his or her work and suggests improvements*

Developmental Factors
(From Levels IV and V of Identification, Discrimination, and Classification Checklist)

The following skills are based on Piaget's theory. They are designed to determine whether the child is able to perform the operations of conservation, reversibility, and seriation, which are associated with the period of concrete operations. The numerals follow the order on the concept development checklist.

Level IV

10.　*Classifies objects by more than one property*
　　　Using a collection of items such as basic shapes in two colors, the child is asked to put the shapes into two groups. The objects can be classified by color or shape. After the child has completed one classification, the

teacher asks the child to organize the objects into groups using a different way.
Example:

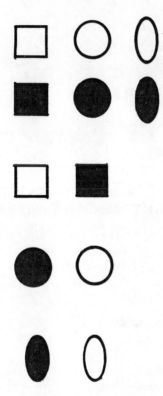

11. *Reverses simple operations: arranges/disarranges/rearranges*
     This activity may be accomplished in several ways using conservation of volume in water and matter (clay balls), or conservation of number in arrangements of objects. In the arrangement of objects, the teacher lines up items in two rows using one-to-one correspondence. The teacher then makes one row longer than the other row and asks the child if both rows still have the same number.

Level V

12. *Seriates (arranges) objects by size*
     The teacher takes a collection of objects that vary in size or some other dimension. The child is asked to put the objects in order. Cuisenaire rods or shapes that come in graduated sizes are examples of materials that can be used.

Example:

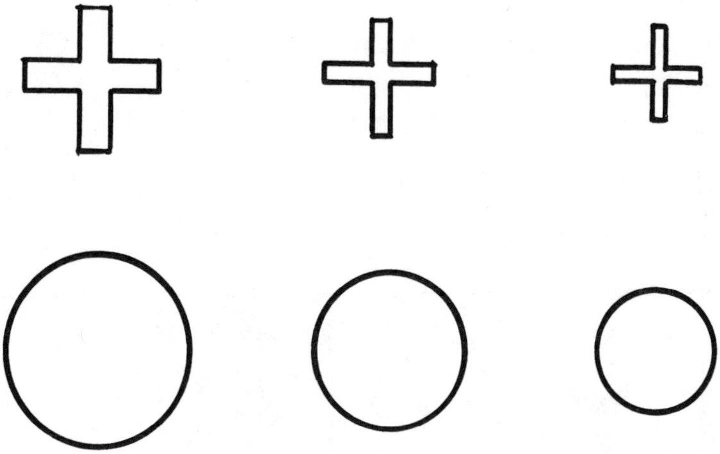

EARLY CHILDHOOD DEVELOPMENTAL CHECKLIST
READING READINESS INSTRUMENT

Auditory Discrimination

1. *Discriminates between similar sounds made by different objects* _____
   Construct three sound jars, two of which contain the same material, such as sand, salt, or rice. The third jar should have a different but similar material. Have the child shake all three jars and select the two that are the same.
       The child pronounces each pair of words accurately after the teacher. The child's back should be to the teacher, or the teacher should conceal his or her lip movements.

2. *Discriminates between initial phonemes* _____

bat/cat _____	spat/scat _____
fat/rat _____	stat/slat _____
plat/flat _____	gat/lat _____
sat/hat _____	vat/wat _____
chat/shat _____	

3. *Discriminates between medial phonemes* _____

bet/bit _____	bot/bet _____
bat/but _____	bate/bite _____
bit/bat _____	bote/bute _____
bin/ban _____	bate/bete _____

4. *Discriminates between final phonemes*   _____

     bat/bam _____   bat/bap _____
     can/cad _____   baf/bas _____
     bet/bed _____   bab/baf _____

Visual Discrimination

5. *Discriminates likenesses and differences in pictured objects, shapes, letters, and words*   _____

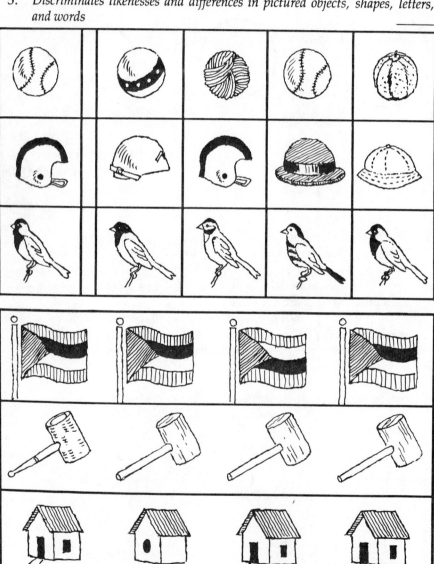

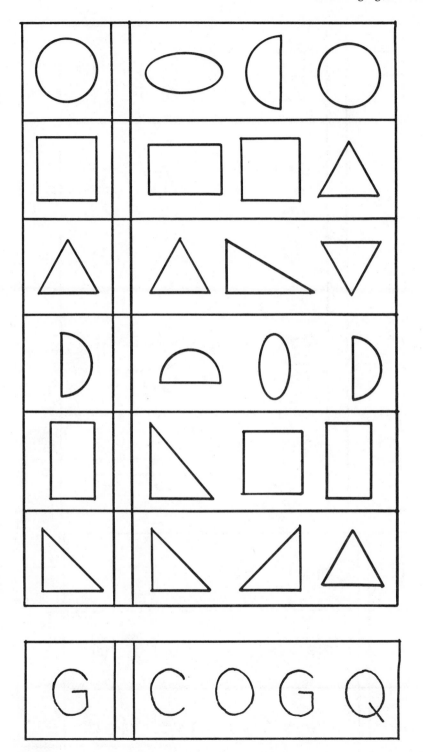

F	E F H T
X	k x W y
i	t j r i
R	P R B S
g	q p g j

at	am	as	at	an
hot	his	hop	hurt	hot
five	live	five	give	fire

week	weak feed peek week
though	through sought though rough

6. *Uses visual memory to match pictured objects, shapes, letters,*
   and words with one removed   _____
7. *Identifies his or her first name in print*   _____
   The teacher prints three or four names, one of which is the
   child's, and asks the child to identify his or her name.
8. *Tracks visually from left to right* (Follows moving object with
   eyes, side to side at reading distance.)   _____
9. *Follows left-to-right progression of a pointer while an adult reads* _____

Letter Knowledge

10. *Matches upper- and lower-case letters*   _____
    The teacher has the child draw a line from upper case to lower case and
    vice versa.

J

D

S

C

L

A

I

a

j

d

s

c

11. *Identifies the letters of the alphabet* _____
    A.   Ask child to find letters as you name them.
    B.   Point to letters in random order. Have the child name the letters.
This activity can be done by letter sound or letter name.

d	v	p	u
a	z	o	e
n	k	m	t
g	y	j	q
x	h	s	w
i	e	b	f
r	l	c	a
S	O	G	A
F	J	I	H

K	C	U	N
R	D	E	Q
W	P	L	T
Y	A	M	X
E	Z	B	V

12. *Arranges letters in alphabetical order* _____
    Use an alphabet puzzle or an alphabet with letters missing.
    Have the child order the letters.
13. *Matches letters with pictures of objects whose names begin
    with the same sound* _____

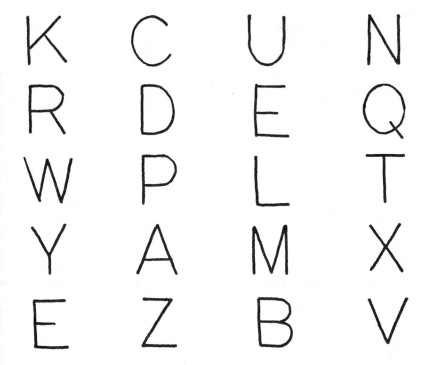

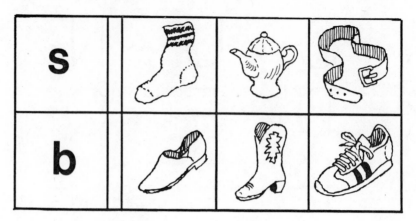

Language and Vocabulary

14. *Listens to and follows verbal directions* _____
15. *Identifies the concept of word* _____
     The child identifies what a word is by drawing a circle
     around a word.

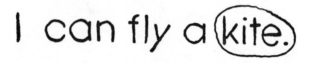

16. *Identifies the concept of letter* _____
     The child identifies what a letter is by drawing a circle around a
     letter in a word.

The (S)oup is hot.

17. *Invents a story for a story book* _____

Oral Comprehension

18. *Locates elements in a picture (tallest, largest and so forth)* _____
19. *Retells in the correct sequence a story read to him or her* _____
20. *Reorganizes pictures to show the correct story sequence* _____
21. *Answers recall questions about a story* _____
22. *Draws analogies from a story to his or her own experience* _____
23. *Makes value judgments about story events* _____

Experience Chart Skills

24. *Tells experiences for an experience story*   _____
25. *Follows left-to-right progression as an adult reads*   _____
26. *Identifies recurring words on an experience chart*   _____
27. *Suggests titles for experience stories*   _____

Fine Motor

28. *Draws circles with closed ends*   _____
    The teacher asks the child to copy the model.

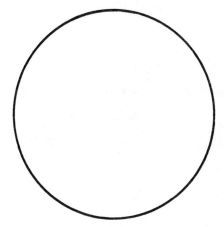

29. *Connects dots with straight pencil lines*   _____
    The teacher draws a model for the child on the first line.

• • • • • • • • • • •

• • • • • • • • • • •

30. *Copies shapes from model*   _____

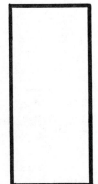 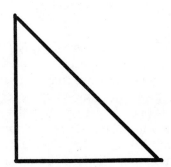

31. *Copies alphabet letters from model* _____

Social-Emotional Factors
(From Level V, Social Play and Socializing Checklist)

1. *Completes most self-initiated projects* _____
2. *Works and plays with limited supervision* _____
3. *Engages in cooperative play* _____
4. *Listens while peers speak* _____
5. *Follows multiple and delayed directions* _____
6. *Carries out special responsibilities (such as feeding animals)* _____
7. *Listens to and follows the suggestions of an adult* _____
8. *Carries out simple errands* _____
9. *Enjoys talking with adults* _____
10. *Can sustain his or her attention span for a variety of duties* _____
11. *Evaluates his or her work and suggests improvements* _____

Developmental Factors
(From Levels IV and V, Identification, Discrimination, and Classification Checklist)

10. *Classifies objects by more than one property* _____
11. *Reverses simple operations: arranges/disarranges/rearranges* _____
   The teacher uses two collections of objects, arranging the items in two rows using one-to-one correspondence. The teacher then makes one row longer than the other row and asks the child if both rows still have the same number.
12. *Seriates (arranges) objects by size* _____
   Using a collection of objects that vary in size or some other dimension, the teacher asks the child to order the objects.

READING READINESS ACTIVITIES

The following activities are designed to promote readiness for reading. In keeping with the young child's need for concrete, manipulative materials, many of the activities use real objects. Other activities have more abstract pictures. Most of the activities are interchangeable for purposes of teaching or evaluating. All activities require the child's active involvement in the learning process.

Auditory Discrimination

Objective 1: Discriminates between similar sounds made by different objects

---

Materials
  Three sound boxes constructed from film cans or small containers. Two boxes contain the same material (oats). The third sound box contains rice.

Activity
  The teacher asks the child to shake all three boxes and select the two that produce the same sound.

Group Size
  Individual

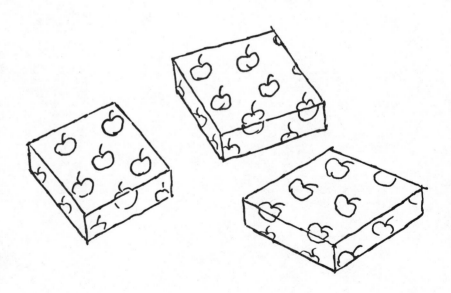

> Objective 5: Discriminates likenesses and differences in pictured
> objects, shapes, letters, and words

Materials

Two sets of self-adhesive pictures of flowers, animals, and so forth purchased from a variety store or stationery shop. Make several sets
of five cards each so that two cards in the set have the same picture. Then make several sets of four cards so that only one card in
the set is different.

A cloth pocket chart constructed with pockets like a shoe holder

Activity

The teacher selects a set of cards from the pocket and the child sorts the
cards, either to find the two that are alike or the one that is different.

Group Size

Individual
Small group

Visual Discrimination

> Objective 5: Discriminates likenesses and differences in pictured
> objects, shapes, letters, and words

Materials

Twenty-four cards made from oaktag. Each card has either a pair of
similar patterns or a pair of different patterns. There should be
twelve cards with the same pattern and twelve cards with different patterns.

Activity

The teacher asks the child to look at the cards and determine whether the
two patterns are the same or different. The child then sorts the cards into
two categories, "same" and "different."

Group Size

Individual

Small group

Objective 5: Discriminates likenesses and differences in pictured
objects, shapes, letters, and words

Materials

A manila folder with a picture of a clown drawn on each side. Some of
the features on the two clowns are the same, other features are
different.

Activity

After examining the two pictures, the child is to identify how the clowns
are alike and how they are different.

Group Size

Individual

Small group

Visual Discrimination

Objective 5: Discriminates likenesses and differences in pictured objects, shapes, letters, and words

---

Materials

    A set of index cards with two pictures to each card. On some cards the pictures are identical, while on other cards the objects are similar or quite different.

Activity

    After a discussion as to the meaning of *same* and *different*, the teacher gives pictured examples of the concept. The child then looks at each card to determine whether the two pictures on the card are the same or are different.

Group Size

    Individual

Objective 5: Discriminates likenesses and differences in pictured objects, shapes, letters, and words

Materials

Pictures cut from magazines of objects familiar to the child
An envelope
A manila folder
Tagboard
Black construction paper

The pictures are mounted on tagboard and cut out. Then the shape of the pictures is traced on black construction paper. These outlines are cut out and glued to the manila folder. The pictures are stored in an envelope that is glued to the back of the folder.

Activity

The child takes the pictures and matches them with the black silhouettes on the folder.

Group Size

Individual
Small group

READING READINESS

Visual Discrimination

Objective 5: Discriminates likenesses and differences in pictured objects, shapes, letters, and words

---

Materials

Several pieces of tagboard cut 2¼″ by 12″. Divide each piece of tagboard into four sections and put a picture of an object, shape, letter, or word in the first section. Put another matching picture in one of the remaining sections and different but similar pictures in two sections.

Activity

The teacher gives the child a strip with instructions to look at the first picture and find the picture that matches from the other pictures on the strip. The process is repeated with each strip.

Group Size

Individual

Small group

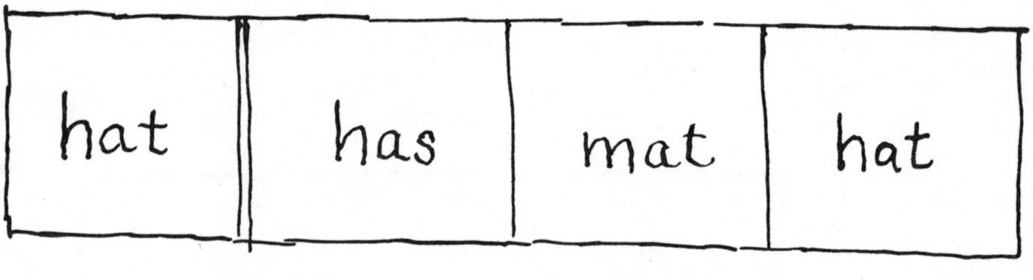

hat	has	mat	hat

Objective 6: Uses visual memory to match pictured objects, shapes, letters, and words with one removed

Materials

Ten squares cut from posterboard 9" x 6"
Ten arrows cut from posterboard
Ten brads
Ten short and long strips of posterboard to serve as flaps

Place a picture at the top of each square and cover it with a short section of hinged posterboard. Place an array of three pictures, one of which matches the picture at the top, at the bottom of the card and cover them with the longer strip of posterboard. The arrow is connected in the center of the card with a brad.

Activity

The child looks at the picture at the top of the card by lifting the flap. After covering the picture, the child then lifts the flap at the bottom of the card and points the arrow to the picture matching the one at the top. The activity can be made self-checking by putting the correct picture on the back of the card or having the child lift the flap at the top of the card to check. The activity can be used with pictures, shapes, letters, and words.

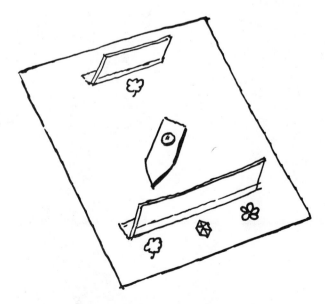

Visual Discrimination

Objective 7: Identifies his or her first name in print

Materials
Names of children printed on cards or an experience chart

Activity
Show each child the card with his or her first name on it. Then show the array of all the names. The child is to pick out the card with his or her name on it.

Group Size
Individual
Small group

Objective 10: Matches upper- and lower-case letters

Materials
> Sets of upper-case and lower-case letters made of plastic, cardboard, and so on combined into six-letter combinations

Activity
> Given the array of letters, the child is asked to match the upper- and lower-case letters

Group Size
> Individual
> Small group

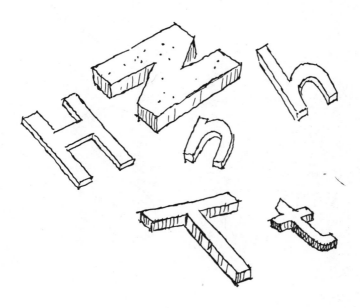

Letter Knowledge

Objective 10: Matches upper- and lower-case letters

Materials
   An egg carton with lower-case letters written in the egg wells
   Plastic eggs with upper-case letters on them

Activity
   The child places the plastic egg in the egg well that has the same letter.

Group Size
   Individual

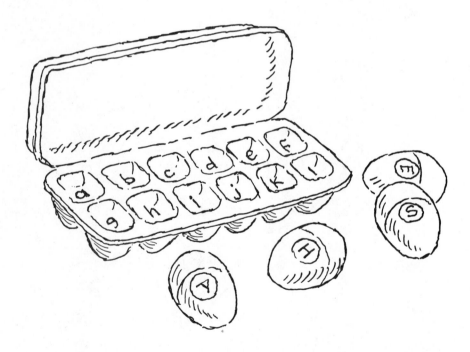

Objective 10: Matches upper- and lower-case letters

Materials
> Two sets of twenty-six flash cards made from index cards, each card with a letter of the alphabet in upper or lower case on it

Activity
> The teacher asks the child to sort the cards by matching the upper- and lower-case letters. If the child is just learning the letters, the cards may be grouped into sets of ten cards with five letters per set.

Group Size
> Individual
> Small group

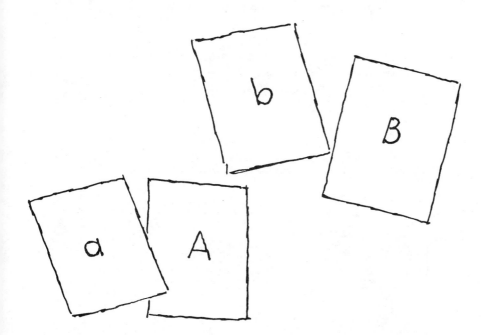

Letter Knowledge

Objective 10: Matches upper- and lower-case letters

Materials
>A manila folder
>A hole punch
>Yarn
>Contact paper
>Masking tape

Write a column of upper-case and lower-case letters in different order on one side of the manila folder. Punch holes to the right of the left-hand column of letters and to the left of the right-hand column of letters. Cut the yarn into lengths of 15 inches. Tape a piece of yarn to the back of the folder and string it through each hole next to the column of letters on the left side of the folder. Wrap the ends of the yarn tightly with tape and cover the back of the folder with contact paper.

Activity
>The child is to take the length of yarn beside the letter on the left side of the folder and find the corresponding letter in the right column. The child then strings the yarn through the hole beside the selected letter.

Group Size
>Independent

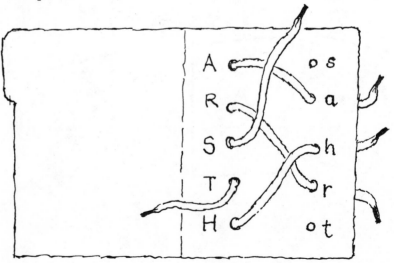

Objective 13: Matches letters with pictures of objects whose
names begin with the same sound as the letter

Materials
> A shoebox made into a mailbox by covering it and the lid with red,
> white, and blue construction paper. Cut a slit in the lid so that
> letters can be dropped into it.
> Twenty-one envelopes with a consonant letter on each
> Small pictures to match each consonant sound

Activity
> The child takes the array of pictures and places each in the envelope with
> the corresponding consonant sound. When all pictures for a sound have
> been found, the child "mails" that envelope (puts it into the shoebox). The
> activity continues until all envelopes have been mailed.

Group Size
> Individual
> Small group

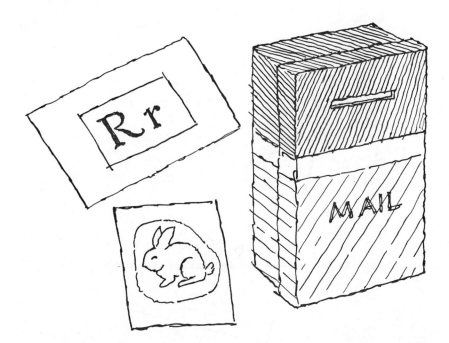

Letter Knowledge

Objective 13: Matches letters with pictures of objects whose
names begin with the same sound as the letter

Materials

A set of picture cards that depict an object with appropriate beginning
consonant sounds
A set of alphabet letters of consonants
Magnetic tape
A magnetic board or other magnetic surface (such as a filing cabinet)

Activity

The teacher attaches strips of magnetic tape to the backs of the pictures
and of the consonant letters. The teacher then asks the child to select
some of the consonant letters and attach them to the metallic surface.
Then the child attaches all pictures corresponding to the selected letters
to the surface below each letter. Letters may be used in small or large
groups.

Group Size

Individual
Small group

Objective 13: Matches letters with pictures of objects whose
names begin with the same sound as the letter

Materials

A carton with twelve dividers constructed to resemble a house or hotel.
Each compartment is labeled with a letter of the alphabet.
Plastic containers with an assortment of pictures of objects that have
the same initial consonant sound as the compartments

Activity

Given an array of objects from several boxes, the child sorts the objects
according to beginning sound and puts them in the correct "room." When
all the objects have been sorted, the child returns the objects to the boxes
for storage.

Group Size

Individual
Small group

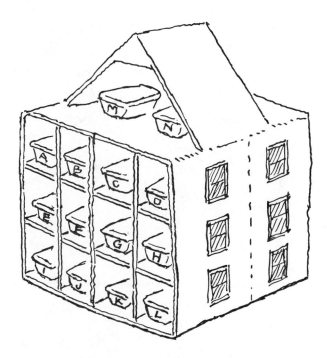

Letter Knowledge

> Objective 13: Matches letters with pictures of objects whose
> names begin with the same sound as the letter

Materials
  Alphabet cards made by gluing flannel letters to tagboard
  Picture cards to match each alphabet letter

Activity
  The teacher asks the child to match the alphabet cards with the appropriate picture. If the child is only beginning to learn sound-to-symbol skills, the cards can be divided up into sets with five or six letter sounds to a set.

Group Size
  Individual
  Small group

Objective 17: Invents a story for a picture book

Materials
Pictures the child selected and cut out.
The pictures are mounted on tagboard and laminated to form a book.

Activity
After the book has been assembled, the child tells the story page by page
as the teacher records it. After the story has been written on the pages,
they are laminated and put together with yarn by the teacher.

Group Size
Individual

Comprehension Skills

Objective 20: Reorganizes pictures to show the correct story
sequence

Materials

Two copies of an inexpensive storybook. Pictures from one copy are
cut out and mounted on tagboard.

Activity

The teacher reads the story to the child. After a discussion of the story, the
child takes the pictures and puts them into the correct sequence. The activity can be made self-correcting by using numerals to indicate the correct order of the pictures.

Group Size

Individual
Small group
Large group

Objective 20: Reorganizes pictures to show the correct story
sequence

Materials
Sets of pictures showing the life cycle of a butterfly, a bird, and a frog,
three cards to each life cycle

Activity
The teacher asks the child to sequence each set of cards in the correct
order.

Group Size
Individual
Small group

Oral Comprehension

Objective 20: Reorganizes pictures to show the correct story
sequence

Materials
Comic strips without words cut apart and glued to tagboard

Activity
The teacher asks the child to use the comic strip sections to sequence the
strips and tell the story.

Group Size
Individual

Objective 30: Copies shapes from a model

Materials
   A small photo album
   Various shapes taped to the left side of the album pages
   A crayon

Activity
   The teacher asks the child to reproduce the shape on each page on the
   facing page of the album

Group Size
   Individual

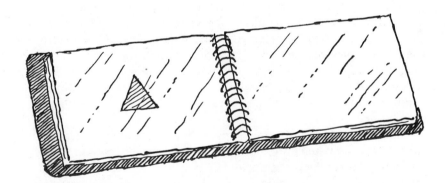

SUMMARY

Most children learn their native language during the years of infancy through early childhood. Not only is language not learned by imitating adult language, it is not taught by adults. Children progress from simple to more complex language using rules of grammar that gradually resemble the language of the community. There are different types of languages called codes, which vary from formal or standard English. Codes may be dialects or different languages, or they may be variations in the level of formality used in the language, depending on the context of conversation. Children learn to switch the code or language form that they use to fit the setting in which they are speaking.

Although adults do not teach children their language in a formal sense, important people in the young child's environment have an influence on the process of language acquisition. Mothers, fathers, and other older individuals simplify their language so that the young child is able to understand what they are saying. Modeling of appropriate language forms, expanding the child's language, questioning and reflecting on the statements made by the child are some of the natural strategies adults use to facilitate a child's language development.

It is uncertain whether the strategies used at home with children are equally effective in a school setting. Although some educators advocate formal language instruction in classrooms, others feel that more natural approaches, similar to the role that parents play in language development, are more effective with young children than are structured language lessons.

Language acquisition is an essential foundation for learning to read. As the child experiences literature and sees written language, he or she becomes aware of the relationship between talking and reading. Parents and teachers who include opportunities for using and expanding language through field trips, storytelling, literature, and discussions facilitate successful reading.

Readiness for reading develops gradually in young children. Educators do not agree on when or how the young child should learn to read. Furthermore, there is similar disagreement on how to determine if the child demonstrates readiness for reading. While some early childhood educators stress social and emotional factors, reading specialists are more concerned with reading readiness skills. Piagetian scholars seek to determine readiness through developmental tasks demonstrating that the child is moving from the preoperations period into the concrete operations period. Whatever philosophy of reading readiness is accepted by the teacher of young children, there are many experiences the teacher can provide to further the child's progress in moving toward reading. Whether the teacher's goal is to include reading instruction, especially for younger children, there are many activities that will provide experiences resulting in growth in language and in a sound foundation for reading.

Almy, M.; Chittenden, E.; and Miller, P. *Young Children's Thinking*. New York: Teachers College Press, 1967.

Bellugi-Klima, U. *The Acquisition of the System of Negation in Children's Speech*. Cambridge, Mass.: MIT Press, 1968.

Berko, J. "The Child's Learning of English Morphology." *Word* 14 (1958): 150–177.

Bernstein, B. *Class, Codes and Control. Vol. 1: Theoretical Studies Toward a Sociology of Language*. Beverly Hills, Calif.: Sage Publications, 1971.

Carroll, J. B. "The Nature of the Reading Process." In Singer and Ruddell, R. (eds.). *Theoretical Models and Processes of Reading*. Newark, Del.: International Reading Association, 1970.

Carrow, E. "Comprehension of English and Spanish by Preschool Mexican American Children." *Modern Language Journal* 55 (1971): 299–306.

Cazden, C. *Language in Early Childhood Education*. Washington, D.C.: National Association for the Education of Young Children, 1972.

Cohen, D. "The Effects of a Special Program in Literature on the Vocabulary and Reading Achievement of Second Grade Children in Special Service Schools." Unpublished doctoral dissertation, New York University, 1966.

Cullinan, B. E.; Jaggor, A.; and Strickland, D. "Language Expansion for Black Children in the Primary Grades: A Research Report." *Young Children* 29 (1974): 98–112.

Doman, G.; Stevens, G. L.; and Orem R. C. "You Can Teach Your Baby to Read." *Ladies Home Journal* 80 (1963): 62.

Downing, J. "The Development of Linguistic Concepts in Children's Thinking." *Research in the Teaching of English* 4 (1970): 5–19.

Dulay, H. C., and Burt, M. K. "Should We Teach Children Syntax?" *Language Learning* 23 (1973): 245–258.

Durkin, D. "When Should Children Begin to Read?" *Innovation and Change in Reading Instruction, Sixty-Seventh Yearbook of the National Society for the Study of Education, Part II*. Chicago: University of Chicago Press, 1968.

Elkind, D. "Cognitive Development and Reading." *Claremont Reading Conference Proceedings*. Claremont, Calif.: Claremont Graduate School, 1974.

Garcia, E. E. "Language Switching in Bilingual Children: A National Perspective." In E. Garcia and M. S. Vargas (eds.). *The Mexican American Child: Language, Cognitive and Social Development*. Tucson: University of Arizona Press, 1981.

Garcia, E. E. "Language Acquisition: Phenomenon, Theory and Research." In B. Spodek (ed.). *Handbook of Research in Early Childhood Education*. New York: Free Press, 1982.

Gibson, E. J. "Learning to Read." *Science* 148 (1965): 1066–1072.

Gleason, J. B. "Do Children Imitate?" *Proceedings of the International Conference on Oral Education of the Deaf*, Washington, D.C.: Alexander Graham Bell Assoc. for the Deaf, June 17–24, 1967, Vol. II, 1441–1448.

Guszak, F. J. *Diagnostic Reading Instruction in the Elementary School*. New York: Harper & Row, 1972.

Huerta, A. "The Development of Codeswitching in a Young Bilingual." *Working Papers in Sociolinguistics* 21 (1977).

Labov, W., and Cohen, P. "Systematic Relations of Standard and Nonstandard Rules in Grammars of Negro Speakers." *Project Literacy Reports No. 8.* Ithaca, N.Y.: Cornell University, 1967.

Lavatelli, C. S. *Language Training in Early Childhood Education.* Urbana, Ill.: University of Illinois Press for the ERIC Clearinghouse on Early Childhood Education, 1971.

Moore, R. S., and Moore, D. N. *Better Late Than Early.* New York: E. P. Dutton, 1975.

Newport E. "Motherese: The Speech of Mothers to Young Children." In N. Castellan; D. Pisoni; and G. Potts (eds.). *Cognitive Theory II.* Hillsdale, N.J.: Lawrence Erlbaum Associates, 1976.

Robinson, V. B.; Strickland, D.; and Cullinan, B. "The Child: Ready or Not?" In L. Ollila (ed.). *The Kindergarten Child and Reading.* Newark, Del.: International Reading Association, 1977, 13–39.

Schachter, F. F., and Strage, A. A. "Adults' Talk and Children's Language Development." In S. G. Moore and C. R. Cooper (eds.). *The Young Child Reviews of Research, Volume 3.* Washington, D.C.: National Association for the Education of Young Children, 1982.

Waller, T. G. *Think First, Read Later!* Newark, Dela.: International Reading Association, 1977.

CHAPTER 6

Play and Social Development

Madame Montessori observed that play is a child's work. It is the key to the young child's growth and learning. This chapter explores the benefits of play for young children. Two facets of play that make important contributions to the child's development, the dramatic and the social, are discussed. The two accompanying checklists, (1) Dramatic Play and (2) Social Play and Socializing, provide suggestions for how the teacher or caregiver can facilitate sociodramatic play and the development of social skills.

THE IMPORTANCE OF PLAY

All children play. Children play alone, with their peers and siblings, and with adults. Play is a spontaneous part of the child's development and a natural function of childhood.

Children need to play. It is their way of making sense of the world in which they live. Although there is a tendency today to deemphasize spontaneous play in educational settings, advocates take a strong position for its merits. Anker (1974) proposes that through play children gain a sense of autonomy and effectiveness and are able to develop self-direction and trust in themselves.

Children also learn through play. Piaget (1952) linked play with cognitive development. Children use play as a vehicle to understand concepts. After mastering or learning a new behavior, the child repeats or practices the behavior as an enjoyable play experience.

Play also has a function in the development of imagination and creativity. Lieberman (1977) calls this development "playfulness." The child who

211

role plays in the early years becomes the adolescent who fantasizes, using imagination in expressive endeavors and in the process of invention.

Children use different kinds of play endeavors as they move through stages of development. As little children grow and mature, their play gradually becomes more complex. Parten (1932) and Barnes (1971) described this growth in levels of social play. Social participation in play increases with the child's age. The young child first plays alone in solitary play and then progresses to parallel play, where he or she plays alongside another child. When the child plays together with other children, associative play has developed. In the highest level, cooperative play, children not only play together, but they are able to plan together for play.

THE ROLE OF DRAMATIC PLAY IN LEARNING AND DEVELOPMENT

Little children love to pretend when they play. The ability to pretend or play make-believe begins in infancy and develops in complexity as the child matures. The child later enjoys using pretend play with other children.

The baby first uses pretend play at about twelve months of age. For the first time the baby is able to use representational thought, such as pretending he or she is sleeping or eating. This is called *symbolic play* because the child is representing or symbolizing an action (Fein, 1982). Later the toddler can pretend that a doll is a baby or that objects represent something. However, at first the objects must be realistic (Fein, 1975). Later, as children grow older they can use less realistic toys for symbolic play.

Symbolic play becomes sociodramatic play when the child is able to respond or interact with another person. At about three years, when the child is moving into Parten's associative and cooperative levels of play, the child begins to engage in sociodramatic play with another child or with a group of children. As in symbolic play, sociodramatic play develops and becomes more complex as the children gain experience. Children are able to discuss what they are playing or pretend they are someone else talking within the sociodramatic play activity (Garvey and Berndt, 1977). Children can develop intricate planning strategies for use of props and materials as they grow in their ability to elaborate on play themes.

THE ROLE OF THE TEACHER IN DRAMATIC PLAY

The teacher is a facilitator of dramatic play. If the teacher is to play a supportive role in children's play, he or she must first understand the benefits of sociodramatic play and advocate its inclusion in early childhood curriculum. Beyond believing in the merits of sociodramatic play, the teacher can structure the classroom and schedule time so that play has an important place in the program.

The classrom environment affects play behaviors. How centers are arranged and equipped can influence the type and quality of sociodramatic play. Witt and Granza (1969) reported that equipment and materials received more use and encouraged more interactive play when positioned in the center of the classroom than when located in a corner. Brenner (1976) found that large areas result in more social and rough-and-tumble play, while small, enclosed areas encourage quiet and solitary play.

The most commonly used indoor areas for dramatic play are the housekeeping and block centers. Kinsman and Berk (1975) suggest that, by combining these two areas, children's play experiences can be expanded because children have greater opportunities for interacting with varied groups of classmates. The materials in these centers must be evaluated and changed frequently to maintain children's interest and their changing ideas for play themes.

Sociodramatic play can also be organized around social studies themes. For example, one school in my community was studying rodeos. The dramatic play room had saddles, wearing apparel appropriate for a rodeo, and oats for the "horses." Occupational play can be fostered by having on hand prop boxes containing play apparatus for the roles of doctor, beautician, cook, teacher, and other occupations in the community. Occupational prop boxes should be rotated frequently; they may also be coordinated with other components of the curriculum.

Too many toys and alternatives in the classroom can affect how much time is spent in sociodramatic play. Smith and Connolly (1972) determined that the availability of toys for individual or group play affect the amount of time children spend in cooperative play. Sponseller and Jaworski (1979) found that if the environment is arranged to encourage construction activities, less cooperative play will occur. The teacher who is sensitive to the variables that affect sociodramatic play will arrange the classroom to emphasize dramatic play at appropriate intervals.

The teacher should participate in children's play as a resource person and facilitator. Wolfgang (1977) suggests that teachers can involve themselves through observations, but also by asking questions, modeling play behaviors, and giving direct suggestions or explicit demonstrations. Researchers (Smilansky, 1968; Rosen, 1974; Singer and Singer, 1974) found that the teachers who introduced a new play theme for several play sessions, encouraged the children to take roles and carry out the theme, and modeled role-playing behavior while taking part in sociodramatic play, were successful in increasing the extent and quality of children's play.

USING THE DRAMATIC PLAY CHECKLIST

The Dramatic Play Checklist traces the child's development in symbolic and sociodramatic play. As a result of using the checklist and observation of children's play, the teacher can determine what kinds of play themes, props, and experiences are appropriate to extend sociodramatic play development.

Unlike the previous checklists having specific activities or tasks that can be used for assessment or evaluation, items on this checklist are assessed informally when children are engaged in play activities. The experiences provided by the teacher to enhance sociodramatic play are not specific activities for a single checklist item but are general opportunities for sociodramatic play that will facilitate the play behaviors described.

FROST WORTHAM DEVELOPMENTAL CHECKLIST

DRAMATIC PLAY
PRESCHOOL*

Color code: Purple

LEVEL III	Introduced	Progress	Mastery
1. Imitates grownups (plays house, store, and so forth)			
2. Expresses frustrations in play			
3. Creates imaginary playmates			
4. Engages in housekeeping			
5. Paints and draws symbolic figures on large paper			
6. Builds simple structures with blocks			
7. Uses transportation toys, people, and animals to enrich block play			
8. Imagines any object as the object he or she wants (symbolic function)			
LEVEL IV			
1. Role plays in the housekeeping center			
2. Role plays some adult occupations			
3. Participates in dramatization of familiar stories			
4. Uses puppets in self-initiated dialogues			
5. Differentiates between real and make-believe			
6. Pretends dolls are real people			
7. Constructs (paints, molds, and so on) recognizable figures			
8. Participates in finger plays			

**FROST WORTHAM DEVELOPMENTAL
CHECKLIST (continued)**

	Introduced	Progress	Mastery
LEVEL V			
1. Role plays a wide variety of roles in the housekeeping center and in other centers			
2. Role plays on the playground			
3. Role plays a variety of adult occupations			
4. Recognizes that pictures represent real objects			
5. Participates in a wide variety of creative activities: finger plays, rhythm band, working with clay, painting, outdoor play, housekeeping, singing, and so forth			
6. Produces objects at the carpentry table and tells about them			
7. Produces art objects and tells about them			
8. Searches for better ways to construct			
9. Builds complex block structures			

*Developed by Joe Frost and Sue Wortham. Used by permission of Joe L. Frost.

**FROST WORTHAM DEVELOPMENTAL CHECKLIST
DRAMATIC PLAY**

Play both reflects and enhances the child's development. In dramatic play, symbolism develops as the child represents actions, people, or objects. When the child plays alone, symbolic play is the result of pretending or make-believe. As the child matures and is able to carry out make-believe themes with other children, sociodramatic play occurs. The Dramatic Play Checklist contains activities that teachers may observe to determine development of symbolic and sociodramatic play in children. It also suggests activities that will encourage growth in dramatic play. The following list describes these activities in greater detail.

LEVEL III

1. *Imitates grownups (plays house, store, and so forth)*
   The child role plays adult activities with which he or she is familiar. The roles are likely to be played independently or in parallel play.
2. *Expresses frustrations in play*
   The child is able to verbalize difficulties encountered in play activities.

3.   *Creates imaginary playmates*
      The child is able to fantasize and invent a companion. Using symbolic thought, the child uses the imaginary playmate to replace a peer.

4.   *Engages in housekeeping*
      The child enjoys carrying out various activities that occur in the home. Cooking, sweeping, and other activities representative of the family members including siblings are carried out in play themes. These activities are likely to be independent in solitary or parallel play.

5.   *Paints and draws symbolic figures on large paper*
      The child uses symbolic thought in representing people or objects when pointing. Although frequently unrecognizable to adults, the forms have meaning for the child.

6.   *Builds simple structures with blocks*
      Playing alone or alongside others, the child uses blocks to represent buildings or other structures.

7.   *Uses transportation toys, people, and animals to enrich block play*
      The child understands that toy figures symbolize the real object. The toys are used to carry out play activities with block structures.

8.   *Imagines any object as the object he or she wants (symbolic function)*
      The child understands and uses representational thought. Because the child is able to symbolize, if a desired toy is not available, the child substitutes another object. For example, a toy bathtub can become a doll bed.

LEVEL IV

1.   *Role plays a wide variety of roles in the housekeeping center and other centers*
      The child continues the use of play themes and roles in a more involved manner.

2.   *Role plays some adult occupations*
      The child is beginning to understand different occupations and is able to characterize some of the activities of these occupations.

3.   *Participates in dramatization of familiar stories*
      The child is able to pretend at being a character in a story. For example, he or she can be a pig in *The Three Little Pigs*.

4.   *Uses puppets in self-initiated dialogues*
      The child enjoys symbolizing and fantasizing using puppets. The child pretends the puppets are talking, invents what they will say, and has them carry out a dialogue.

5.   *Differentiates between real and make-believe*
      The child is beginning to understand the difference between reality and fantasy. The child knows that cartoon characters do not really exist.

6.   *Pretends dolls are real people*
      The child uses dolls to symbolize people he or she knows. A doll in the

housekeeping center may be used to represent the baby in his or her family.

7. *Constructs (paints, molds, and so on) recognizable figures*
    Constructions, paintings, and drawings are used to represent people, toys, or pets. These representations are more accurate than those made at Level III.

8. *Participates in finger plays*
    The child takes part more frequently in group activities in dramatic play. He or she uses symbolism through finger plays.

LEVEL V

1. *Role plays in the housekeeping center*
    As in Level III the child carries out housekeeping roles, but with more complexity. The child is able to carry out the roles in more detail and depth.

2. *Role plays on the playground*
    Role playing now includes outdoor play. Using larger play spaces, the child extends sociodramatic play with exercise.

3. *Role plays a variety of adult occupations*
    The child understands that people engage in many different occupations. Role playing of occupations and other roles demonstrates the child's growth in sociodramatic play and understanding of home and community.

4. *Recognizes that pictures represent real objects*
    The child has moved to a more abstract level of symbolism. Whereas the younger child needed realistic objects for representation, the older child now understands pictures to serve the same purpose.

5. *Participates in a wide variety of creative activities: finger plays, rhythm band, working with clay, painting, outdoor play, housekeeping, singing, and so forth*
    The child participates fully in all classroom play activities.

6. *Produces objects at the carpentry table and tells about them*
    The child uses advancing motor development skills to construct representations at the carpentry table and is able to describe the representations.

7. *Produces art objects and tells about them*
    The child increases the use of creativity in fashioning art objects and is now able to describe these representational creations.

8. *Searches for better ways to construct*
    Imagination and problem solving are used to design and construct objects using a variety of large and small materials.

9. *Builds complex block structures*
    The child demonstrates growth in motor development and sociodramatic play development through complex block structures representing a variety of kinds of buildings, rockets, ramps, and so on used to carry out play themes.

THE ROLE OF SOCIAL PLAY AND SOCIALIZING
IN LEARNING AND DEVELOPMENT

Piaget described toddlers as egocentric, unable to understand the views of others. Parten likewise described very young children's play as solitary. The child might be physically near other children, but his or her play does not involve interaction with other children. As development continues and the child becomes more aware of the perspectives of peers, social relationships can become part of the child's play.

Peer play provides children with opportunities to understand other views or thoughts. Within group play activities children become able to express their own viewpoints and hear the views of their friends. It is through peer play that the child learns and tries out new social skills.

As the child moves into associative and cooperative levels of play, he or she develops social abilities. The child entering group play experiences must learn how to be accepted by peers and to maintain peer relationships. For the first time children must acquire social strategies that will enable them to be part of a group of children.

At about age four a first task for preschool children when they are new to a group is to become acquainted with the other children. Children who are successful at doing this are likely to suggest an activity that includes other children, or they may suggest playing with other children. Children who are unsuccessful at becoming acquainted depend on the teacher to help them (Asher and Renshaw, in preparation). Another problem for preschoolers is to be accepted in an ongoing play activity. Corsaro (1978) noted that socially successful children gain peer acceptance by observing the activity and then integrate themselves into the activity by behaving as the other children are behaving. Another strategy suggested by popular or successful children is to wait until there is a break in a game and then join in.

Once accepted into peer play, children must be able to maintain social relationships. Successful children use friendly social behavior, such as giving things to another, submitting to another's wishes, or giving affection (Hartup, Glazer, and Charlesworth, 1967). Children who use negative behavior, such as noncompliance, aggression, or attack, particularly in conflict situations, are not successful in maintaining peer relationships.

Preschool children are in the process of learning acceptable social behaviors through practice. Because they cannot yet discriminate between acceptable and unacceptable social behaviors, they use both in their play (Baldwin, 1948). Those who have learned to understand the perspective or viewpoint of other children tend to have developed their positive social skills better.

THE ROLE OF THE TEACHER IN SOCIAL PLAY AND SOCIALIZING

The teacher plays an important role in children's social development. As in sociodramatic play, arrangement of the environment and availability of toys affect social play. Teacher guidance and instruction can also facilitate the development of positive social behaviors.

Sociodramatic play and outdoor play provide the best opportunities for social interaction among children. House and doll play, puppet play, or play in a block center are more conducive to peer play than are individual activities such as easel painting or table activities. The provision of too many toys hinders interaction. When there is a limited amount of equipment or materials, children spend more time talking to each other (Doke and Risley, 1972).

Teachers can facilitate positive social behaviors by using both indirect and direct teaching strategies in the classroom. Teachers can also suggest appropriate strategies to children and make them aware of the consequences of negative behavior. Three direct actions teachers can use are reinforcing, modeling, and coaching. *Reinforcing* is giving positive approval to a child or children who are using the desired play behaviors or approximations of them. In *modeling* the correct or positive behavior is demonstrated for the child. Peers, films, and teachers can all role play or model effective social behaviors for children who lack the skills. *Coaching* involves telling the child the best social behaviors for different situations. Although this strategy is more difficult with younger children because it uses abstract ideas, it has been used successfully (Oden and Asher, 1977).

There is more to the development of social skills than maturation. Children develop social skills both through their own attempts and with the assistance of perceptive adults. The Social Play and Socializing Checklist traces this development through examples of activities and behaviors that reflect the child's use of positive social behaviors.

USING THE SOCIAL PLAY AND SOCIALIZING CHECKLIST

The Social Play and Socializing Checklist provides indicators of the child's social development. By observing the child's ability to understand the perspectives of others and to translate this knowledge into positive social interactions, the teacher can use the checklist in two ways to facilitate social play. First, the checklist can serve as a guide for organizing center materials and dramatic play settings that will allow children to try out their social skills with their peers. Second, using the checklist to indicate desired social behaviors, the teacher can use modeling, coaching, reinforcement, or suggestions in his or her own behaviors to facilitate the child's acquisition of desired behaviors that have not yet been developed.

FROST WORTHAM DEVELOPMENTAL CHECKLIST

SOCIAL PLAY AND SOCIALIZING
PRESCHOOL*

Color code: Green

LEVEL III	Introduced	Progress	Mastery
1. Engages in independent play			
2. Engages in parallel play			
3. Plays briefly with peers			
4. Recognizes the needs of others			
5. Shows sympathy for others			
6. Attends to an activity for ten to fifteen minutes			
7. Sings simple songs			
LEVEL IV			
1. Leaves the mother readily			
2. Converses with other children			
3. Converses with adults			
4. Plays with peers			
5. Cooperates in classroom routines			
6. Takes turns and shares			
7. Replaces materials after use			
8. Takes care of personal belongings			
9. Respects the property of others			
10. Attends to an activity for fifteen to twenty minutes			
11. Engages in group activities			
12. Sings with a group			
13. Is sensitive to praise and criticism			
LEVEL V			
1. Completes most self-initiated projects			
2. Works and plays with limited supervision			
3. Engages in cooperative play			
4. Listens while peers speak			
5. Follows multiple and delayed directions			
6. Carries out special responsibilities (for example, feeding animals)			
7. Listens and follows the suggstions of adults			

**FROST WORTHAM DEVELOPMENTAL
CHECKLIST (continued)**

	Introduced	Progress	Mastery
8. Enjoys talking with adults			
9. Can sustain an attention span for a variety of duties			
10. Evaluates his or her work and suggests improvements			

*Developed by Joe Frost and Sue Wortham. Used by permission of Joe L. Frost.

**FROST WORTHAM DEVELOPMENTAL CHECKLIST
SOCIAL PLAY AND SOCIALIZING**

As the young child develops the ability to understand the thoughts and needs of others, he or she is able to play within a group of children and have concern for the problems or needs of friends. The checklist provides indicators of the child's development of social relationships and responsibility. Below is a description of the checklist objectives to assist teachers in determining the social play behaviors of their children.

LEVEL III

1. *Engages in independent play*
   The child plays by herself, either alone or in a group of children.
2. *Engages in parallel play*
   The child plays in proximity to other children. Although children may be engaged in similar play activities, there is no interaction between the children.
3. *Plays briefly with peers*
   The child makes tentative interactions with other children while involved in play activities.
4. *Recognizes the needs of others*
   The child is beginning to understand the perspective of another child. His or her behavior demonstrates knowledge of another child's needs or desires.
5. *Shows sympathy for others*
   The child shows by action or conversation that he or she is concerned for another child's distress. The child is acquiring altruism.
6. *Attends to an activity for ten to fifteen minutes*
   The child is able to stay with an activity rather than frequently changing from one activity to another. Concentration on a task is developing.
7. *Sings simple songs*
   The child is able to participate briefly in singing activities.

LEVEL IV

1. *Leaves the mother readily*
   The child demonstrates confidence in managing new social situations and is able to leave his or her mother or another caregiver without apprehension.

2. *Converses with other children*
   The child is developing social interaction skills. The child is able to express views and acknowledge the thoughts of others.

3. *Converses with adults*
   The child has developed the confidence to express thoughts to adults.

4. *Plays with peers*
   The child is playing more frequently with another child or a group of children. The child tries out various social skills.

5. *Cooperates in classroom routines*
   The child understands and carries out responsibilities as part of a group of children.

6. *Takes turns and shares*
   The child recognizes that social relationships with peers require positive social behaviors. The child is able to respond to others' needs and desires most of the time.

7. *Replaces materials after use*
   The child accepts responsibility by following classroom routines when using play materials.

8. *Takes care of personal belongings*
   The child takes care of clothing and other personal possessions that are used at school.

9. *Respects the property of others*
   One of the indicators that a child is acquiring social skills is his or her understanding of property rights. The child is developing an appreciation that some things are not for use without permission.

10. *Attends to an activity for fifteen to twenty minutes*
    The child's attention span is lengthening. He or she is able to maintain interest in an activity.

11. *Engages in group activities*
    The child is gaining confidence in belonging to a group. He or she feels comfortable in participating with the group.

12. *Sings with a group*
    The child enjoys singing with others. He or she is expressing the ability to interact socially in various group activities.

13. *Is sensitive to praise and criticism*
    The child understands that his or her behavior affects others. The child recognizes that praise and criticism are responses to successful or unsuccessful social behaviors.

LEVEL V

1. *Completes most self-initiated projects*
   The child shows perseverance in attending to activities by completing one activity before moving on to another.
2. *Works and plays with limited supervision*
   The child is becoming more successful in social play interactions. The child's behaviors are becoming more dependable.
3. *Engages in cooperative play*
   The child is able to participate fully in group play. He or she can now plan and carry out play themes with a group of peers.
4. *Listens while peers speak*
   The child understands that maintaining social relationships requires responding to the views and perspective of others. The child knows that it is important to listen to others as well as expressing his or her own ideas.
5. *Follows m le and delayed directions*
   The child is able to accept being given responsibilities to carry out and can follow several directions without difficulty.
6. *Carries out special responsibilities (for example, feeding animals)*
   The child enjoys taking responsibility on a regular basis and takes pride in doing well with responsibility on a regular basis.
7. *Listens and follows the suggestion of adults*
   The child is sensitive to adult advice and is aware that following adult suggestions brings positive results.
8. *Enjoys talking with adults*
   The child is developing more confidence in relationships with adults and can carry on conversations in a relaxed manner.
9. *Can sustain an attention span for a variety of duties*
   The child understands that daily routines require various changes in activities. The child is able to respond appropriately to jobs that occur during the course of the day.
10. *Evaluates his or her work and suggests improvement*
    The child not only accepts evaluations made by others but is perceptive of how well an activity has been completed. The child can determine how improvement can be made in future efforts.

SUMMARY

Play is important for the child's development. Through play the child gains a sense of direction, and develops cognition and creative thinking skills. Various theorists have explained how play reflects development. Each theory describes the child's play as starting with a focus on self and evolving gradually to include other children.

When the infant is able to use representation in thoughts and actions, pretend play or symbolic play emerges. In symbolic play the child pretends he or she is doing something make-believe with toys. Later the child is able to use pretend play with other children. This interactive make believe is called sociodramatic play. As children gain experience in symbolic and sociodramatic play, their play becomes more complex and elaborate.

Social play and socializing are related to the child's ability to initiate and maintain relationships with other children. Before a child can move away from egocentrism, or self-focus, the child has to be able to understand the views of others. In becoming more aware of the perspectives of others, the child learns that others have their own thoughts, which differ from the child's own. As this awareness grows, social relationships also become part of the child's play. Frequent experiences in peer play help the child develop social skills.

The young child must learn how to use strategies in social play that will gain peer acceptance. Preschool children must learn how to become acquainted in a new situation, how to be accepted into changing play situations, and how to manage conflicts that arise during play.

To maintain social relationships with peers, the child learns which play behaviors are successful. Although all young children use both negative behaviors, such as aggression, which result in rejection, and positive behaviors, which are more successful, most children learn to use positive social behaviors.

The teacher has an important role in facilitating sociodramatic play and the development of social skills. One of the teacher's responsibilities is to organize the learning environment to facilitate the development of social relationships through sociodramatic play. The block and housekeeping center are central to encouraging group play. Activities that are group oriented, rather than individual, will also foster group experiences.

Another variable the teacher manages is time management. Sociodramatic play and social skill development are facilitated best if the teacher schedules time for play both indoors and outdoors.

Materials and equipment provided in the learning setting also influence group play. Prop boxes for role playing, puppets, and materials associated with social studies themes enhance children's interest in organizing and implementing group play activities.

The teacher can also have a more directive role in sociodramatic play and the development of social skills. When children are engaged in play, the teacher can make suggestions on how play themes can be elaborated or changed. The teacher may also offer suggestions to a child on which play behaviors will help gain group acceptance.

In some instances the teacher may use teaching strategies with children who are having difficulty in sociodramatic play. The teacher may initiate a play theme and demonstrate roles to show children how to carry out play ideas. Similarly, the teacher may instruct children who are unsuccessful when playing in how to use positive play behaviors in various play settings with other children.

The teacher learns the sociodramatic play characteristics and social skills of her or his children by observing them at play. Using the Dramatic Checklist and the Social Play and Socializing Checklist, the teacher may determine the child's growth in play behaviors. From the guidelines provided by the checklists, the teacher can plan room arrangements and materials and also choose teacher behaviors that will foster growth in sociodramatic and social play skills in young children.

REFERENCES

Anker, D., et al. "Teaching Children as They Play." *Young Children* 29, 4 (1974): 203–213.

Asher, S. R., and Renshaw, P. D. "Social Skills and Social Knowledge of High- and Low-Status Kindergarten Children." In preparation.

Baldwin, A. L. "Socialization and the Parent-Child Relationship." *Child Development* 19 (1948): 127–136.

Barnes, K. "Preschool Play Norms: A Replication." *Developmental Psychology* 51 (1971): 99–103.

Brenner, M. "The Effects of Sex, Structure, and Social Interaction on Preschoolers' Make-Believe in a Naturalistic Setting." 1976 (ERIC Document Reproduction Service No. ED 128 103).

Corsaro, W. A. *"We're Friends Right?" Children's Use of Access Rituals in a Nursery School.* Working Papers in Sociolinguistics. Austin, Texas: Southwest Educational Development Laboratory, 1978.

Doke, L., and Risley, T. R. "The Organization of Day-Care Environments: Required vs. Optional Activities." *Journal of Applied Behavior Analysis* 5 (1972): 405–420.

Fein, G. "A Transformational Analysis of Pretending." *Developmental Psychology* 11 (1975): 291–296.

Fein, G. "Pretend Play: New Perspectives." In J. F. Brown (ed.). *Curriculum Planning for Young Children.* Washington, D.C.: National Association for the Education of Young Children, 1982.

Garvey, K., and Berndt, R. "Organization of Pretend Play." *Catalog of Selected Documents in Psychology* 7 (1977): 1589.

Hartup, W. W.; Glazer, J. A.; and Charlesworth, R. "Peer Reinforcement and Sociometric Status." *Child Development* 38 (1967): 1017–1024.

Kinsman, C. A., and Berk, L. E. "Joining the Block and Housekeeping Areas: Changes in Play and Social Behavior." *Young Children* 35, 1 (1975): 66–75.

Lieberman, J. N. *Playfulness: Its Relationship to Imagination and Creativity.* New York: Academic Press, 1977.

Oden, S., and Asher, S. R. "Coaching Children in Social Skills for Friendship Making." *Child Development* 48 (1977): 495–506.

Parten, M. "Social Participation Among Preschool Children." *Journal of Abnormal and Social Psychology* 27 (1932): 243–369.

Piaget, J. *Play, Dreams and Imitations in Childhood.* New York: Norton, 1952.

Rosen, C. E. "The Effects of Sociodramatic Play on Problem-Solving Behavior Among Culturally Disadvantaged Preschool Children." *Child Development* 45 (1974): 920–927.

Singer, J. L., and Singer, D. G. "Enhancing Imaginative Play in Preschoolers: Television and Live Adult Effects." 1974 (ERIC Document Reproduction Service No. 100 509).

Smilanksy, S. *The Effects of Sociodramatic Play on Disadvantaged Preschool Children.* New York: Wiley, 1968.

Smith, P. K., and Connolly, K. J. "Patterns of Play and Social Interaction in Preschool Children." In N. B. Jones (ed.). *Ethological Studies of Child Behavior.* Cambridge: At the University Press, 1972.

Sponseller, D., and Jaworski, J. "Social and Cognitive Complexity in Young Children's Play: A Longitudinal Analysis." Paper presented at the Annual Meeting of the American Educational Research Association, San Francisco, 1979.

Witt, P. A., and Granza, A. F. "Position Effects and Play Equipment Preferences of Nursery School Children." Springfield: Illinois State Department of Mental Health, 1969 (ERIC Document Reproduction Service No. ED 045 185).

Wolfgang, C. *Helping Aggressive and Passive Preschoolers Through Play.* Columbus, Ohio: Charles E. Merrill, 1977.

CHAPTER *7*

Motor Development

One of the major tasks facing infants and toddlers is mastering the use of their bodies, especially learning to walk. The early childhood years are spent further developing motor skills. This chapter discusses how young children develop motor skills and how the teacher and school environment can affect motor development. The Motor Development Checklists for gross and fine movement provide the teacher with indicators of milestones in physical growth.

HOW CHILDREN DEVELOP MOTOR SKILLS

Young children spend a great portion of every day in active, physical activities. As they participate in play, they are developing their gross and fine motor skills. Fine motor skills result from movements requiring precision and dexterity. Putting a puzzle together or learning to write, which are manipulative tasks, are fine motor skills. Gross motor skills are those involving movements of the entire body or major parts of the body. Locomotor skills, which are major body movements such as walking, running, and jumping, require gross motor skills. Some tasks, such as throwing a ball accurately, require both fine and gross motor skills (Malina, 1982).

Most motor skills have developed by six or seven years of age (Espenschade and Eckert, 1974). Although all children develop motor skills in the same sequence, they vary in the rate and proficiency of development. Many factors can influence motor development: low birth weight, poor nutrition, and obesity can delay the development of motor skills. Nor is the development of motor proficiency a consistent or smooth progression. In addition to individual differences in development, there are also differences within individual children. Children may perform differently on the same task from time to time.

There are also differences in development that can be attributed to the sex of the child. In the early childhood years boys are better at running, jumping, and throwing activities, while girls do better in hopping activities (Espenschade and Eckert, 1974). Social class differences and parent expectations for children may affect differences in motor development. Eleanor Maccoby and Carol Jacklin (1974) found that mothers treat sons differently from daughters from the time their children are infants. Malina (1973) reported that children from lower socioeconomic backgrounds might be given greater freedom to play in the neighborhood, which could promote opportunities to practice motor activities. Conversely, Emmy Werner (1972) found that the cultural practices in some cultures of physically restraining infants with clothing can delay motor development.

IMPLICATIONS FOR EDUCATION

Although there is general agreement that the opportunity to engage in physical activities promotes the development of motor skills, there are opposing views on the role of the teacher. While some educators advocate allowing the child free choices of play as the mode for acquisition of motor skills, others believe the teacher should direct specific activities that will require the child to use desired movements.

Some writers have designed programs that provide activities in perceptual-motor education, neurological organization, and sensory integration. Participation in these programs is expected to correct motor deficiencies and remedy academic functioning. Although reviewers such as Libby Goodman and Donald Hammill (1973) and Myers and Donald Hammill (1976) have indicated that motor development programs have not had a significant influence on the motor capacities of children, other studies, including those of Zema Schaney et al. (1976) and Peter Werner (1974), have proposed that carefully planned programs for motor development do have a significant positive influence on motor behavior. Bryant Cratty (1982) has proposed that carefully designed studies are needed to determine more clearly the effectiveness of programs containing movement experiences.

Opponents of structured programs in movement education believe the teacher's role is to provide opportunities for motor development through free play. The child is permitted to explore and choose activities that will foster the development of fine and gross motor skills in both indoor and outdoor play areas. Through choices of manipulative and locomotor activities the child has opportunities for physical exploration and discovery and practice of motor skills.

Children play naturally when given the opportunity. If the classroom and playground contain various kinds of equipment and materials, children will be practicing motor skills as they engage in various play activities.

The indoor play environment should contain a variety of manipulative toys such as puzzles, pegboards and pegs, and small construction toys. The art center is full of possibilities for fine motor development. Painting, drawing, exploring with clay, and other art activities provide for creativity, as well as the use of manipulative skills.

The block center provides opportunities for motor development. Children can build with large and small blocks and maneuver transportation toys in the course of play. Children using the block center are exercising both large and small muscles.

The outdoor play environment allows children to develop gross motor skills as they run, climb, swing, and slide. As the child initiates physical activities on the playground, he or she is developing skill in using increasingly complex physical actions. The child is also making discoveries about spatial relations such as laterality and directionality.

The type of outdoor play environment available for children's play has an impact on the type of play activities that can take place. In past years playgrounds consisted of metal equipment such as swings, slides, merry-go-rounds, and seesaws. While this type of playground was adequate for exercise play, newer creative playgrounds promote social and creative play in addition to motor development.

Creative playgrounds contain multipurpose climbing structures. These consist of a platform with various entries and exits such as ramps, tire climbers, cargo nets, fire-fighter poles, and slides. In addition to various types of motor activities, the structure encourages sociodramatic play and fantasy play as the child uses make believe to transform the structure into a ship, a fire station, or a house. Horizontal tire swings, vehicle paths, and open areas are all conducive to active play that will enhance motor development.

Whether the teacher has an organized motor development program, the daily schedules should include many opportunities for indoor and outdoor play that will permit the children to make choices about their play activities. As they paint at the easel, contruct block towers, ride a tricycle, or slide down a fire-fighter's pole, they are developing gross and fine motor skills.

USING THE MOTOR DEVELOPMENT CHECKLISTS

The motor development checklists provide indicators of the child's development in gross and fine motor skills. The skills listed are not comprehensive but provide examples of the skills children develop at each level. The checklist is meant to be used as an observational tool for the teacher to use when children are at play. In some skills, such as bouncing and catching a ball, the teacher might introduce the activity to evaluate or encourage development of the skills.

FROST WORTHAM DEVELOPMENTAL CHECKLIST

MOTOR DEVELOPMENT
PRESCHOOL*
Gross Movement

Color code: Blue

LEVEL III	Introduced	Progress	Mastery
1. Catches a ball with both hands against the chest			
2. Rides a tricycle			
3. Hops on both feet several times without assistance			
4. Throws a ball five feet with accuracy			
5. Climbs up a slide and comes down			
6. Climbs by alternating feet and holding on to a handrail			
7. Stands on one foot and balances briefly			
8. Pushes a loaded wheelbarrow			
9. Runs freely with little stumbling or falling			
10. Builds a tower with nine or ten blocks			
LEVEL IV			
1. Balances on one foot			
2. Walks a straight line forward and backward			
3. Walks a balance beam			
4. Climbs steps with alternate feet without support			
5. Climbs on a jungle gym			
6. Skips haltingly			
7. Throws, catches, and bounces a large ball			
8. Stacks blocks vertically and horizontally			
9. Creates recognizable block structures			
10. Rides a tricycle with speed and skill			
LEVEL V			
1. Catches and throws a small ball			
2. Bounces and catches a small ball			
3. Skips on either foot			

FROST WORTHAM DEVELOPMENTAL CHECKLIST (continued)

	Introduced	Progress	Mastery
4. Skips rope			
5. Hops on one foot			
6. Creates Tinkertoy and block structures			
7. Hammers and saws with some skill			
8. Walks a balance beam forward and backward			
9. Descends stairs by alternating feet			

*Developed by Joe Frost and Sue Wortham. Used by permission of Joe L. Frost.

FROST WORTHAM DEVELOPMENTAL CHECKLIST
MOTOR DEVELOPMENT

Gross Movement

LEVEL III

1. *Catches a ball with both hands against the chest*
   When thrown a medium-sized ball, the child catches it with both hands. Attempts at catching are awkward and not always successful.
2. *Rides a tricycle*
   The child can manage pedaling and steering fairly well. There may be some difficulty in maneuvering turns.
3. *Hops on both feet several times without assistance*
   The child still needs the security of both feet to maintain balance.
4. *Throws a ball five feet with accuracy*
   The child is developing throwing skills. The child can throw overhand, usually with some accuracy.
5. *Climbs up a slide and comes down*
   The child manages the steps of a slide and the transition to sitting on the slide without difficulty.
6. *Climbs by alternating feet and holding on to handrail*
   When climbing stairs the child is able to use alternating feet rather than bringing both feet together on each step before climing to the next one.
7. *Stands on one foot and balances briefly*
   This skill may not occur naturally in play. The teacher may ask the child to stand on one foot to check for balance.
8. *Pushes a loaded wheelbarrow*
   The child is able to balance the wheelbarrow while lifting and propelling it.

9. *Runs freely with little stumbling or falling*
    The child now has well-developed locomotor skills and runs with few signs of awkwardness.
10. *Builds a tower with nine or ten blocks*
    The child is able to build and balance a tower of blocks.

LEVEL IV

1. *Balances on one foot*
    Balance is better established. The child can stand on one foot for several seconds.
2. *Walks a straight line forward and backward*
    The child can use alternating feet to walk along a line on the ground.
3. *Walks a balance beam*
    Balance is maintained when walking forward on a balance beam.
4. *Climbs steps with alternate feet without support*
    The child can walk up and down steps without using a handrail.
5. *Climbs on a jungle gym*
    The child uses both arms and legs to manage a jungle gym or geodesic dome climber.
6. *Skips haltingly*
    The child is beginning to use skipping skills, but usually is awkward in his or her attempts.
7. *Throws, catches, and bounces a large ball*
    The child accomplishes throwing and catching with consistent accuracy and tries some bouncing.
8. *Stacks blocks vertically and horizontally*
    The child can balance both large and small blocks.
9. *Creates recognizable block structures*
    The child has mastered the skill of arranging and stacking blocks and is able to plan and build structures.
10. *Rides a tricycle with speed and skill*
    The child has mastered all the skills required for riding a tricycle and manage any maneuver required to operate it.

LEVEL V

1. *Catches and throws a small ball*
    The child has graduated from using a medium-sized or large ball to a small ball. Catching and throwing skills are more precise.
2. *Bounces and catches a small ball*
    The child can not only bounce a ball but is also able to catch the ball with consistency.
3. *Skips on either foot*
    Skipping movements have improved. The child practices skipping with both feet.

4. *Skips rope*
   The child attempts rope-skipping activities with some success.
5. *Hops on one foot*
   Balancing has improved. The child can manage several hops with either foot.
6. *Creates Tinkertoy and block structures*
   Structures are elaborate and may combine several construction sources.
7. *Hammers and saws with some skill*
   The child explores workbench tools and is able to use a hammer and saw, though with some awkwardness.
8. *Walks a balance beam forward and backward*
   The child's balance while walking on a balance beam has improved. The child is able to manage a variety of balance beam actions.
9. *Descends stairs by alternating feet*
   The child is able to walk downstairs using both feet and may not need to use the handrail.

FROST WORTHAM DEVELOPMENTAL CHECKLIST

MOTOR DEVELOPMENT
PRESCHOOL*
Fine Movement

Color code: Blue

LEVEL III	Introduced	Progress	Mastery
1. Places small pegs in pegboards			
2. Holds a paintbrush or pencil with the whole hand			
3. Eats with a spoon			
4. Buttons large buttons on his or her own clothes			
5. Puts on a coat unassisted			
6. Strings beads with ease			
7. Hammers a pound toy with accuracy			
8. Works a three- or four-piece puzzle			
LEVEL IV			
1. Pounds and rolls clay			
2. Puts together a five-piece puzzle			
3. Forms a pegboard design			
4. Cuts with scissors haltingly and pastes			

FROST WORTHAM DEVELOPMENTAL CHECKLIST (continued)

	Introduced	Progress	Mastery
5. Eats with a fork correctly			
6. Holds a cup with one hand			
7. Puts a coat on a hanger or hook			
8. Manipulates large crayons and brushes			
9. Buttons buttons and zips zippers haltingly			
LEVEL V			
1. Cuts and pastes creative designs			
2. Forms a variety of pegboard designs			
3. Buttons buttons, zips zippers, and ties shoes			
4. Creates recognizable objects with clay			
5. Uses the toilet independently			
6. Eats independently with a knife and fork			
7. Dresses and undresses independently			
8. Holds and manipulates pencils, crayons, and brushes of various sizes			
9. Combs and brushes hair			
10. Works a twelve-piece puzzle			

*Developed by Joe Frost and Sue Wortham. Used by permission of Joe L. Frost.

FROST WORTHAM DEVELOPMENTAL CHECKLIST
MOTOR DEVELOPMENT

Fine Movement

LEVEL III

1. *Places small pegs in pegboards*
   The child explores using a pegboard. Most of the child's effort is spent in mastering the activity.
2. *Holds a paintbrush or pencil with the whole hand*
   The child grasps a paintbrush or pencil in her or his fist and uses large movements when painting or drawing.
3. *Eats with a spoon*
   The child grasps a spoon with the whole fist and is able to eat unassisted with little difficulty.
4. *Button large buttons on his or her own clothes*
   The child can manage large buttons on the front of clothing.

5. *Puts on a coat unassisted*
   The child is able to put his or her arms in a coat and pull it on.
6. *Strings bead with ease*
   The child uses fine motor movements in pushing a string through beads and moving them to the end of the string.
7. *Hammers a pound toy with accuracy*
   Hammering movements are precise and accurate.
8. *Works a three- or four-piece puzzle*
   The child is developing figure-ground perception and is able to use contour and shape to work a puzzle.

LEVEL IV

1. *Pounds and rolls clay*
   The child uses hand and finger movements to manipulate clay.
2. *Puts together a five-piece puzzle*
   The child is able to attend to more detail in puzzles.
3. *Forms a pegboard design*
   The child has mastered the task of using a pegboard and has moved to planning and implementing designs using repetition of color or line.
4. *Cuts with scissors haltingly and pastes*
   The child uses scissors awkwardly and has difficulty using the correct amount of paste or glue.
5. *Eats with a fork correctly*
   The child can use the fork with fair precision and does not have to use the whole fist.
6. *Holds a cup with one hand*
   The child can drink liquid from a cup holding the cup in one hand with little spilling.
7. *Puts a coat on a hanger or hook*
   The child can hang his or her coat more easily on a hook and can manage a hanger fairly well.
8. *Manipulates large crayons and brushes*
   The child holds crayons and brushes correctly, but movements may still be somewhat awkward.
9. *Buttons buttons and zips zippers haltingly*
   The child manages buttons and zippers on the front of clothing with some difficulty.

LEVEL V

1. *Cuts and pastes creative designs*
   The child has mastered cutting and pasting and can now use these skills to make interesting compositions.
2. *Forms a variety of pegboard designs*
   The child's designs are now elaborate and complex.

3. *Buttons buttons, zips zippers, and ties shoes*
    The child has mastered most of the skills required for putting on and taking off clothing, although she or he may have some trouble manipulating back zippers or buttons.

4. *Creates recognizable objects with clay*
    The child has mastered movements to manipulate clay and enjoys creating representational figures.

5. *Uses the toilet independently*
    The child is able to remove and replace clothing and use the toilet appropriately.

6. *Eats independently with a knife and fork*
    The child is able to use a knife and fork, though with some awkwardness.

7. *Dresses and undresses independently*
    The child is able to manage most dressing skills without adult assistance or supervision.

8. *Holds and manipulates pencils, crayons, and brushes of various sizes*
    The child has a pretty good mastery of fine movement skills. Writing may be too difficult, but less precise movements are manageable.

9. *Combs and brushes hair*
    The child uses a comb and brush but with some awkwardness in movements.

10. *Works a twelve-piece puzzle*
    The child can construct more complex puzzles using improved perceptual skills.

SUMMARY

One of the major accomplishments of the early childhood years is the development of motor skills. From birth until about seven years of age the infant, toddler, and young child are in the process of mastering gross and fine motor skills.

Development of motor skills results from the child's active involvement in activities that exercise both gross and fine motor movements. While running, jumping, and climbing the child uses locomotor skills. When painting, working with clay, or putting together a puzzle, the child is using manipulative or fine motor skills. Progress in acquiring motor skills is not always consistent. A child may do well in throwing a ball one day, but exhibit some difficulty the next. However, over a period of time and with practice, motor skills continue to improve.

The teacher's role in helping children develop motor skills is important, but there is uncertainty over the advisability of using a structured program for motor development. Experts disagree on whether motor development programs provide any advantage in children's acquisition of motor skills.

Whether the teacher uses an organized curriculum for motor development, she or he can provide many opportunities for using gross and fine motor skills, both indoors and on the playground. In the classroom, art activities, manipulative materials such as puzzles and pegboards, and block-center activities can be made available on a daily basis. Outdoors, a creative playground with a multipurpose climbing structure, wheel toys, swings, and open areas for active play will enhance the acquisition of fine and gross motor skills.

A child plays by choice. If the teacher provides time, appropriate materials, and equipment for indoor and outdoor play, the child will make play choices that will lead to the natural development of motor skills.

REFERENCES

Cratty, B .J. "Motor Development in Early Childhood: Critical Issues for Researchers in the 1980's." In B. Spodek (ed.). *Handbook of Research in Early Childhood Education*. New York: Free Press, 1982.

Espenschade, A., and Eckert, H. "Motor Development." In W. R. Johnson and E. R. Buskirk (eds.). *Science and Medicine of Exercise and Sport*, 2nd ed. New York: Harper & Row, 1974.

Goodman, L., and Hammill, D. "The Effectiveness of the Kephart-Getman Activities in the Developing Perceptual-Motor and Cognitive Skills." *Focus on Exceptional Children* 4 (1973): 121–126.

Macoby, E. E., and Jacklin, C. N. *The Psychology of Sex Differences*. Stanford University Press, 1974.

Malina, R. M. "Ethnic and Cultural Factors in the Development of Motor Activities and Strength in American Children." In G. L. Rarick (ed.). *Physical Activity: Human Growth and Development*. New York: Academic Press, 1973.

Malina, R. M. "Motor Development in the Early Years." In S. G. Moore and C. R. Cooper (eds.). *The Young Child Reviews of Research, Volume 3*. Washington, D.C.: National Association for the Education of Young Children, 1982.

Myers, P. I., and Hammill, D. *Methods for Learning Disorders*, 2nd ed. New York: Wiley, 1976.

Schaney, Z.; Brekke, B.; Landry, R.; and Burke, J. "Effects of a Perceptual Motor Training Program on Kindergarten Children." *Perceptual and Motor Skills* 43 (1976): 428–430.

Werner, E. E. "Infants Around the World: Cross-Cultural Studies of Psychomotor Development from Birth to Two Years." *Journal of Cross-Cultural Psychology* 3 (1972): 111–134.

Werner, P. "Education of Selected Movement Patterns of Pre-School Children." *Perceptual and Motor Skills* 39 (1974): 795–798.

CHAPTER **8**

Getting Started

If individualized instruction is to be used in the early childhood classroom, the teacher needs not only to organize materials to prepare for instruction but also to prepare the environment and the children for an increased amount of student self-direction. Organization is the key word because all facets of the instructional process must be carefully planned and arranged in order for diagnostic and prescriptive instruction to function smoothly. Several sequential steps pave the way to getting started in individualizing instruction. These steps are organizing the materials, organizing the environment, preparing the children, conducting the initial assessment, implementing instruction, planning with the children, and implementing ongoing diagnosis and assessment. Each of these steps is discussed below.

ORGANIZING THE MATERIALS

The initial step in organizing instruction for diagnostic and prescriptive teaching is to evaluate and arrange the materials to match the checklist, which serves as the curriculum framework. Teachers who are comfortable with the use of purchased kits and curriculum guides perceive the reorganization of teaching resources to be a formidable task. Indeed, to completely revise the curriculum materials for different uses does take time; however, it does not all have to take place in a single school year. Also, the teacher can recruit parents or other sources of volunteer time to assist in the task.

Constructing an Assessment Inventory

Familiarity with the developmental checklist is a prerequisite to organizing resources. The first step in material organization is to determine how each activity is to be assessed. Some objectives will require an activity, while others may be evaluated through teacher observation. Descriptions in previous chapters explain what is involved for evaluating student mastery of objectives. At the early childhood level, teachers often find it useful to write the assessment activity and needed materials for each objective on a file card and then place the file-card box and materials in a large cardboard box. Because the same objects can often be used to assess more than one objective, the teacher can select the needed materials from the total collection. Other teachers prefer to organize the assessment activity with instructions and materials in separate containers. These can be shoe boxes or purchased storage systems. Activities such as the ideas included in this volume are often used to assess a skill. Assessment activities may be teacher constructed or collected from kits or other commercial sources. Assessment activities should be coded to the checklist.

Inventorying and Coding Commercial Materials

After an assessment system has been completed, resources for teaching objectives must be evaluated and coordinated. This process is never finished because the teacher will be adding new resources to the existing system from time to time. As an initial procedure the teacher should study the available commercial resources and programs.

Commercial resources vary from excellent to poor. Teachers often purchase them because they are attractive and colorful, rather than because they are educationally sound. Within the process of inventorying commercially produced materials, the teacher should investigate how and why the materials were produced. Do the materials have a theoretical basis or rationale in their design? What approach to early childhood education is the basis for their design and manufacture? Have the materials been tested with children to assure effectiveness? Are the materials developmentally appropriate? The teacher needs to be knowledgeable about the value of the materials he or she has purchased. If the kit or materials are not compatible with the teacher's approach to teaching young children, they should not be used just because they are available.

In the course of assessing and evaluating the materials and kits, the teacher matches activities that are well designed to the appropriate objective on the checklist. Single materials can be coded individually. In the case of a kit of materials, the appropriate codes can be placed on the outside of the box.

As part of the process of inventorying and evaluating materials, teachers can develop a resource system. Figure 1 demonstrates how one might be developed. In the first column the teacher records activities from commer-

FIGURE 1. CURRICULUM RESOURCE SYSTEM

CATEGORY: QUANTITATIVE AND PROBLEM SOLVING
Level IV Objective 4: Understands the concepts of *first* and *last*

Teacher-Directed Activities	Independent Activities	Other Resources

cial resources, such as teacher guides or idea books. Teacher-designed lessons are also included. The activity, the source, and where it is located are all recorded. The second column contains all the games, center activities, and teacher-made materials to be used by a child or group of children without teacher direction. Again, the source of the materials and page number or location are indicated. The third column is used for resources that do not necessarily fall into the first two categories. A lesson recorded by the teacher for a listening center is an example of an activity that would be recorded in the third column. Group games that might be used as reinforcing activities in an informal setting, rather than as a formal lesson, might also fit into the last column.

Initially the teacher records already existing commercial resources and teacher-prepared activities. As more activities are located or constructed, the teacher may add these also.

ORGANIZING THE ENVIRONMENT

Although the use of learning centers or areas is not a requirement in diagnostic-prescriptive instruction, teachers find them to be helpful if students are to engage in self-directed or independent activities. Some consideration needs to be given to how the room can be arranged so that quiet areas are not adjacent to noisier ones, how traffic will flow, where materials will be stored when not in use, and how children will know the procedures for using learning activities.

The design of the learning environment varies in every classroom depending on the physical nature of the area and the style of the teacher. Before arranging the room, the teacher should determine how many centers will be used, what kinds of materials can be used in the centers, and where the best locations are for centers. Although preschool teachers are expected to have center arrangements, many primary teachers are not accustomed to using them as part of the classroom instruction. Many resources are available to assist the teacher who has had little or no experience with learning centers. Some recommended resources are *Young Children in Action: A Manual for Preschool Educators*, by Hohmann, Banet, and Weikart; *Early Childhood Education: A Guide for Observation and Participation*, by Lindberg and Swedlow; and *One at a Time All at Once: The Creative Teacher's Guide to Individualized Instruction Without Anarchy*, by Blackburn and Powell. These and many other publications offer ideas and assistance in organizing the classroom environment. Although such information will not be reproduced here, the arrangement of the environment is an important component in the implementation of individualized instruction.

After plans have been made for center design and the classroom has been arranged, the teacher is ready to establish guidelines for use of the centers. The teacher undertakes a careful analysis of each area to determine when, how, and where the students may use materials. The teacher also includes instructions on how to remove and return materials correctly. Although not all possible problems can be avoided, the teacher tries to anticipate difficulties students might face while working in the centers and to eliminate or minimize them before children encounter them.

The teacher studies the centers and learning areas and establishes guidelines or rules for each before the school year begins. After school has begun and the children are involved in center activities, the teacher may solicit their input on how center use may be refined and guidelines changed as needed.

Finally, organization of the learning environment includes training the children in learning center procedures. As part of the orientation given to children during the first weeks of school, the teacher teaches them how to use the centers, providing guidelines for each center and then opportunity for practicing center procedures under supervision.

PREPARING THE CHILDREN

The manner in which students are oriented to the classroom environment and routines during the first weeks of school can be predictive of how well the students will manage their behaviors and activities for the entire year. Planning for the beginning orientation becomes as specific as determining which objectives should be included on a checklist of skills. As the orientation progresses, the teacher constructs additional checklists for classroom routines. Before working with the children to help them acquire the desired classroom behaviors, the teacher studies classroom processes to determine the behaviors he or she will expect from the children.

First to be considered are the classroom routines. The teacher lists the routines the children must learn, such as bathroom procedures, walking and talking in the classroom, or carrying chairs from one location to another. The list of items that children need to know to function effectively in the classroom should be exhaustive, in that every possible procedure or routine is included.

Next, the teacher thinks about each item on the list and writes the necessary behaviors for each procedure or routine. One classroom routine is the procedure children follow when they arrive at school. When children arrive they hang up their sweaters or coats, put away their lunch boxes or give their lunch money to an adult, and so forth. The teacher considers all the behaviors in this routine and determines how each task should be completed successfully. The next step is to decide how to teach the children each part of the arrival routine. The teacher thinks through the kinds of activities that will be used to insure that children understand the desired behaviors for the routine.

It is very important that teachers not assume that children enter school knowing how to use the correct behaviors. This mistake often results in children behaving inappropriately. A better approach is to assume that children *do not* know the desired behaviors and must be taught each one.

A final step is to determine when and how to orient the children to the behaviors for each routine of the school day. During the first weeks of school the teacher should demonstrate the routines, have the children practice and role play them, and make sure they have mastered each to the teacher's satisfaction. The teacher should observe the children carrying out each routine and check that procedure off the list when all children are performing it satisfactorily. Children who are having difficulty with a routine should have it retaught to them and should demonstrate it again for the teacher. Just as children differ in their pace of cognitive learning, they also differ in their rate of acquiring classroom routines. Some will need more reinforcement than others.

Guiding children in the use of areas or centers in the classroom follows the same steps as with classroom routines. First, the teacher lists all behaviors needed in order to use each center. In the manipulative center, for example, the teacher must determine where each piece of material is to be used. Are puzzles to be used on a table or a rug? How are the puzzles to be carried? Are puzzle pieces to be taken out of the frame, or may they be turned over and dumped out? How are the puzzles to be returned to the shelf? After analyzing all these activities and listing the behaviors, the teacher has the children practice them until assured that each child can use the center appropriately. Teachers often feel they are neglecting important instruction time by spending several weeks showing children how to use the centers, but this is one instance when overteaching can be very productive in the long run. If all children demonstrate that they can and will use the centers appropriately, the teacher is freed from having to conduct constant, close supervision and can expend more of his or her energy in working with the children.

In showing children how to use the centers the teacher also has to determine how many centers to introduce at one time. Some teachers prefer to set up one center and limit children to use of that one center until children are comfortable with the required procedures. Other teachers prefer to organize the entire classroom, introduce the children to several centers, and rotate use of the centers until all are mastered. Children who demonstrate mastery are allowed to work independently while the teacher gives individual attention to children who are still having difficulty.

Orienting children to the learning centers is never a finished process. Each time the teacher introduces new materials in a center, he or she must orient the children to their proper use. Also, after a period of time the students sometimes gradually slip into inappropriate behaviors. In this case the teacher should "recycle" the children through instruction for proper center use until the correct behaviors are again in evidence.

Each time the teacher shows children how to function independently, in a self-directed manner, the overall purpose is being served of helping children to accept responsibility. The teacher wants not only to enhance classroom management but also to transfer ownership of classroom behavior from the teacher to the students. The more students accept responsibility for their involvement in daily activities, the more the teacher is released from imposing disciplinary measures on them. The goal is a smoothly functioning community where positive interactions between the members have developed from the practices the teacher has taught and used to organize the group.

CONDUCTING THE INITIAL ASSESSMENT

Once children have learned how to function with some independence in the classroom environment, the teacher can begin initial assessment using the checklist. Depending on the checklist being used and on the kind of activity involved, assessment can be accomplished through individual or group activities, or by observation of students rather than administering as assessment activity. (For information on observation strategies, see Appendix B.)

Strategies for Assessment

The key to successful assessment that is not overly time consuming is to keep it as simple as possible. For assessment some portions of the checklist are best used with observation of children at play, either indoors or outdoors. The Social Play and Socializing Checklist and the Motor Development Checklists are used for observation. While children are engaged in center or other play activities, the teacher observes behaviors for a few minutes as part of her or his interaction with the children. The teacher picks two or three children to observe and checks items on the checklist or notes them on a pad of paper. What kind of play does the child prefer? Has the child indicated development of all the social interactions at Level III? At Level IV, which relationships are in evidence? Does the child share and take turns? Which relationships are not in evidence? The teacher marks the checklist for the children she is observing on a given day. On succeeding days the teacher will in turn observe other groups until all children have been observed; then the process is repeated. If there are aides or parents available, they can assist in the observation process. At all times the teacher is developing observation skills, which include assessment without interference with ongoing activities.

Gross and fine motor development can also be assessed by using observation. Many of the gross movements occur naturally during outdoor play. Again, the teacher selects several children to study and spends a few minutes observing those children during the play period. In some instances an activity may have to staged so that motor skills can be observed. For example, the teacher may have to initiate activities with balls in order to observe a child's skills in throwing and catching. With a few minutes of observation each day, the teacher is able to determine the progress of motor development for each of the children.

The checklist involving concept development may require individual assessment. Objectives on the math checklist are sometimes assessed in this manner. The teacher gathers a set of activities for each level of the checklist. While children are working in centers, the teacher works with one child at a time, assesses all of the objectives at Level III, and records the results of the child's responses to the tasks at that level. After each child has been assessed, children who have demonstrated mastery at Level III are now assessed on Level IV. Children who need instruction at Level IV are grouped together for instruction. Assessment continues until the teacher has determined a stopping point for each child.

When initial assessment for one area of instruction has been completed, the teacher groups the children for instruction, and small-group instruction commences. When one checklist has been completed for initial assessment, the next area of concept development can be initiated for assessment.

For the best use of time, group assessment is more desirable than individual assessment and should be done whenever possible. Some concepts can be assessed as a part of group activities. The teacher collects enough materials for a group of five activities. As the activities are conducted, the teacher notes which children can successfully complete them and which children are unsure of themselves. When the results are unclear for some children, group activities may be followed by individual assessment. Activities may also be placed in the centers and assessment carried out as the teacher and children work together in the center.

The reading readiness skills that can be assessed using language experience activities are especially suited to group assessment. When language experience activities are conducted daily, the teacher may include activities such as identifying recurring words in the experience story. As children make individual responses to the activity, the teacher may note which children have achieved the skill and which children need more experiences with it.

The biggest difficulty teachers have in conducting assessments for the first time is that it becomes too time consuming. They get discouraged because the task seems endless and instruction is delayed. There are some strategies teachers can use until they develop short cuts of their own.

1. Avoid overassessing at the beginning of the year. Assessment should cease when the child has reached a level of frustration. If a child misses several objectives, the teacher may stop. It is not necessary to continue

assessment for an entire level of objectives if it is obvious that the child needs to have instruction at that level.

2. Assess in groups whenever possible. Assess individually only when an individual response is necessary.

3. Avoid assessing at too low a level. If you have indications that a child can work at a higher level, assessment should begin at that level. Assessment time can be save by skipping levels when the teacher is certain the child can do those objectives.

4. "Steal" time from other activities and use small sections of time for assessment. If some of the children do not sleep at nap time, that time may be used for individual work. If there is an aide available or another adult who works with the children, squeeze in assessment activities while children are washing their hands for lunch or are engaged in some activity that does not require the teacher's supervision.

Arrival time may be used for assessment. As children arrive in the morning, a few assessment activities may be completed before other children require the attention of the teacher.

Efficient management of time makes initial assessment seem easier. If the teacher maintains a flexible role in the classroom and looks for assessment opportunities, diagnosis does not become a problem at the beginning of the school year. When the teacher has a picture or profile of each child's abilities and needs, individualized instruction can proceed.

Developing a Student Profile

As the process of assessment progresses, a picture of each student begins to emerge from the checklists. The teacher is able to determine how various components of the child's development affect and interact with each other. As the teacher compares the child's progress on various aspects of development, clearer indications of strengths and weaknesses suggest the kinds of experiences that will be most helpful in facilitating learning and growth.

Developing a Master Chart

To be able to plan for each student within the context of the total group of students, the teacher develops a profile of the class from the individual profiles. To accomplish this, a master chart is constructed using the checklist objectives with information for the entire class. Results from individual checklists are transferred to the master checklist. Figure 2 shows how a classroom of children would be represented on a master chart of the Quantitative and Problem-Solving Checklist. With the development of the master chart, the teacher can expedite grouping of children for instruction.

FIGURE 2. MASTER CHART

MATH: QUANTITATIVE AND PROBLEM SOLVING

LEVEL III

	Mario	Frank	Janet	Sue Ellen	George	Miles	Annette	Ben	Mary Blanche
1. Manipulates and experiments with simple machines	+	+	+	+	+	+	+	+	+
2. Counts by rote from 1 to 5	+	+	+	−	+	−	+	+	+
3. Forms creative designs with materials	+	+	+	+	+	+	+	+	+
4. Uses construction materials for multiple purposes	+	+	+	+	+	+	+	+	−
5. Perceives objects from different visual perspectives	+	+	+	+	+	+	+	+	+

LEVEL IV

	Mario	Frank	Janet	Sue Ellen	George	Miles	Annette	Ben	Mary Blanche
1. Counts by rote from 1 to 10	−	+	+	−	−	−	+	+	−
2. Demonstrates the concept of number through 5	−	+	+	−	−	−	+	+	−
3. Orders the numerals 1 to 5	−	−	+	−	−	−	+	+	−
4. Understands the concept of *first* and *last*	−	−	+	−	−	−	+	+	−
5. Identifies:									
a) penny			+				+	+	
b) nickel			+				−	−	
c) dime			+				+	+	
6. Compares differences in dimension (taller/shorter, longer/shorter, thinner/wider)			+						
7. Demonstrates one-to-one correspondence			+						

Grouping Students by Common Needs

After studying the master chart, the teacher is ready to form groups for instructions. Although Figure 2 represents only a small portion of a class, examples of groups can be demonstrated as follows:

(1)   Level III, objective 2: Counts by rote from 1 to 5
       Sue Ellen   Miles
(2)   Level IV, objective 1: Counts by rote from 1 to 10
       Mario   Sue Ellen
       George   Miles
       Mary Blanche
(3)   Level IV, objective 5b: Identifies: nickel
       Annette   Ben

IMPLEMENTING INSTRUCTION

When students have been grouped by objective, the teacher plans for instruction. Using resources of activities for each objective to be taught, a series of teacher-directed and independent activities are selected for each group. The teacher places appropriate materials in the learning center and conducts preliminary planning with the class.

As part of the daily plan the teacher alternates formal and informal teaching activities with time to work with children in problem solving or conversation. Because the teacher giving individual instruction is no longer teaching the class as a group or moving small groups through the same curriculum, management of instructional time is preplanned to assure that the needs of all children are met.

The model of classroom management presented here is based on the assumption that the child is an innate learner and within a carefully arranged environment is able to initiate learning. Most learning is intrinsic, and the role of the teacher is to facilitate that learning. A second assumption is that the child learns through play or acting on the environment. A third assumption is that learning occurs between peers, and from exposure to many experiences; therefore, even though a checklist is used, the child is also processing information and learning concepts that have not been taught formally nor introduced in a prescribed sequence. Although this philosophy may seem to be at odds with a curriculum based on a sequenced checklist, both can be compatible in implementation.

The management procedure adopted in this approach to child learning includes blocks of time during the day when children are free to select and work in centers, arts areas, and other prepared interest areas, as well as working with the teacher. The teacher's role as facilitator of learning means that she or he will engage in direct instruction, interaction in the centers, and informal conversations with children as they explore materials in the classroom. The teacher will also participate in ongoing routines such as finding needed materials or helping solve problems encountered by children during the work period.

In planning activities for a given instructional period when the teacher's focus will be on math, prior study of the master plan and objectives on the math checklist permits the teacher to form a framework for how instructional time will be spent. With an awareness of how children have been grouped, specific math materials have been placed in the math center to provide reinforcing activities for some children while the teacher conducts initial direct instruction for children beginning another objective. Implied in this planning is that each child will have some time for self-selected activities, while a portion of the time will be spent engaged in direct instruction or evaluation with the teacher or in informal center-reinforcement activities.

As a result of planning for children's needs and surveying available materials, the teacher's master plan might include the following strategies for one instructional period:

8:30–8:45　Work in math center with children learning to count (Level III, objective 2—Counts by rote from 1 to 5).

8:45–9:00　Floating time. Observe children at work in various centers throughout the learning environment. Ask questions about activities.

9:00–9:15　Conduct introductory lesson with children on number concept (Level IV, objective 2—Demonstrates the concept of number through 5). Construction of sets to match numerals from 1 to 5.

9:15–9:30　Floating time. Observe children to determine whether individual children need guidance in moving to new activities.

9:30–9:45　Follow-up lesson for children learning to construct sets (Level V, objective 7—Compares elements of unequal sets). Give the children collections of objects and ask them to make sets that are equal and unequal. Note children who seem to have mastered the objective and who are ready to move on.

Obviously, the indicated time periods are flexible. The teacher may lengthen or shorten any of the activities as the instructional period progresses.

PLANNING WITH THE CHILDREN

Any management strategy used by a teacher that includes student involvement in self-selected and -initiated activities also involves students in planning for the working period. Daily planning with children not only allows the teacher to share her or his plans for the period with the children, but gives the children an opportunity to consider the projects or activities in which they wish to engage.

Before the work period begins, the teacher meets with the children as a group and discusses her or his plans for the period. The teacher tells groups approximately when she will be meeting with them and what activities have been planned for them. Materials and activities that are available in the centers are also discussed. The teacher asks the children in turn to discuss their plans for the work period. Some children may be given specific assignments in addition to center activities they propose to pursue. The period becomes for each child a balance between structure and informality within an environment full of possibilities.

As part of the planning for the work period, the teacher reminds the children not to disturb the teacher while a lesson is being conducted and reviews ways to signal for help if they encounter difficulty and immediate assistance is not available.

Before the planning time ends, each child makes a verbal plan for the work period. Children who are indecisive or who have not yet demonstrated that they are able to make a plan are guided by the teacher with suggestions and instructions for use of the centers. Later during floating periods the teacher checks with each child to determine what progress is being made in planned activities. Prior to moving to another center, children having difficulty completing activities receive consistent attention to reinforce their efforts at finishing the tasks they have selected.

After the work period has been completed, the children have an opportunity to share their experiences with the teacher and fellow students. The activities of the period are discussed before the teacher and class move into another segment of the school day.

IMPLEMENTING ONGOING DIAGNOSIS AND ASSESSMENT

As a result of the development of formal and informal evaluation strategies for ongoing diagnosis, the teacher is able to maintain instruction for individual children throughout the school year. Ongoing diagnosis and assessment means that, once the teacher has completed an initial assessment, grouped children for instruction, and initiated activities to help children master objectives, assessment of their progress will be continuous.

Because assessment does not mean that instruction ceases when evaluation is needed, continuous diagnosis throughout the year is built into ongoing direct instruction or informal learning activities. Essentially, the teacher uses all of the experiences planned for children to keep tabs on what progress the children are making. Some of the following conditions can provide the teacher with ongoing diagnosis and assessment.

1. *Culminating activities that are planned in a structured lesson led by the teacher.*
    As a final assessment, after a series of formal and informal experiences have been provided over a period of time, the teacher involves the chil-

dren in an activity that will allow her or him to determine whether the child exhibits mastery of a concept.

2. *Observation of children working in centers, either with materials to which they have been assigned, or as a result of incidental observations of self-selected activities involving the concept being studied.*

3. *Activities designed in a game format that are partially conducted by the teacher or other adults and that require using the concept for successful participation in the game.*

   Game activities can be led by students, parents, aides, and so forth, who can provide feedback to the teacher when needed.

4. *Formal assessment at the end of instruction of a single objective, or to conduct a periodic "checkup" on a series of objectives.*

   The teacher may want to use an occasional instructional period to conduct assessment activities to verify the child's understanding of a series of objectives that have been checked off as a result of informal assessments over a period of time. Hopefully, this approach to assessment will be used least frequently so that assessment is not time consuming. A natural interaction with children that would be more productive in the long run is always a preferred evaluation strategy.

Regrouping of Children

As a natural process of diagnosis, instruction, and ongoing assessment, the grouping of children at the beginning of the year usually is a very temporary arrangement. Children tend to be inconsistent in their pace of learning. In addition, young children attending school for the first time succumb to colds, viruses, and childhood diseases that result in frequent absences. Consequently, grouping of children must be flexible and will frequently change, as some children advance more rapidly than others and some children for one reason or another need more reinforcement of a skill. Some children will also demonstrate the need for a slower-paced progress more comfortable for their style of learning. Whatever the cause for indicated changes, the teacher will regroup whenever necessary. Occasionally, when it is warranted, some children may be functioning in more than one group. The teacher's acceptance and expectation that frequent regrouping is a natural part of instruction will do much to make flexible groups a little noticed process in classroom routines.

Recordkeeping

With the trend of increasing accountability to parents, school administrators, and state and federal agencies, recordkeeping becomes a necessary evil for teachers, who are required to, or desire to have individual records on children based on curriculum checklists.

Records are useless if they are not kept up to date. In some districts where records of individual progress are kept for parent conferences or visits by official representatives of state and federal programs, up-to-date record-keeping lends validity to the teacher's effectiveness in providing for individual needs and knowledge about the children in the classroom. Parents who drop in for an informal or scheduled conference are reassured when the teacher can explain the curriculum being used and give specific examples of how the individual child is mastering specific concepts.

Teachers who are determined not to let recordkeeping become unmanageable invent strategies to keep them from getting behind. One method that has proved successful is to have the master profile of the class accessible during work periods. As the teacher is teaching or observing the children, changes in progress that need to be recorded are noted immediately at the end of a lesson or during a transition period. Other teachers prefer to keep a small pad and write down items to be recorded at the end of the day. Regardless of the method used, teachers who have successful recordkeeping systems record progress on master checklists as frequently as every day and update individual student records once a week, or no less frequently than every other week.

If recordkeeping is completed less frequently than every two weeks, some negative effects tend to occur. Often the teacher becomes discouraged by the amount of clerical work and feels the system is unworkable or that demands for recordkeeping are unreasonable. Another consequence is that the teacher is not as alert to student progress and tends to revert to the use of large-group instruction as the only instructional mode. Mastery of checklist objectives is then recorded as an assumption rather than as a result of demonstrated behaviors. Having worked with teachers who are successful with management of recordkeeping, it has been my observation that it can be done successfully without undue pressure on the teacher. Teachers new to the process find that, after an initial period of learning how to keep track of the children, less and less time is spent keeping records. I found this to be my own experience as a classroom teacher. Conversely, teachers who are convinced that recordkeeping is a difficult task usually find their expectations fulfilled. Teacher attitude has much to do with success or failure with recordkeeping.

When recordkeeping is implemented as a natural part of the teaching process, it becomes a powerful tool for short- and long-term planning. As more teachers adopt recordkeeping and share its advantages with their peers, teachers are becoming less apprehensive when faced with the requirement of including it as part of their instructional responsibilities. Recordkeeping can be a positive addition to effective teaching.

SUMMARY

Reactions to individualization of instruction through the use of a checklist of skills have been positive or negative depending on the educator's philosophy about a structured curriculum in the early childhood classroom. Many early childhood specialists are rightfully concerned that the structured checklist will result in a rigid, academically oriented preschool classroom that will require children to attend to fragmented tasks rather than promote creative, child-initiated experiences. Although a checklist of objectives does impose a framework for curriculum development, it is not intended to replace the sound practices that preschool teachers have employed for generations of children.

The utilization of a curriculum framework that helps the teacher determine developmentally appropriate activities is suitable in an early childhood classroom. Early childhood educators have long espoused the importance of preparing a rich environment for young children to explore; however, the definition of such an environment is often vague. Children are entitled to learn in an environment where materials have been selected purposefully by a knowledgeable teacher, rather than as a random collection of toys and materials known to be commonly used in preschool programs. A developmental checklist permits the teacher to blend creative activities, which include music, art, dramatics, and play, with a curriculum that recognizes and responds to children who come to school with diverse experiences, abilities, and interests.

REFERENCES

Blackburn, J., and Powell, W. *One at a Time All at Once: The Creative Teacher's Guide to Individualized Instruction Without Anarchy*. Pacific Palisades, Calif.: Goodyear Publishing, 1976.

Hohmann, M.; Banet, B.; and Weikart, D. *Young Children in Action: A Handbook for Preschool Educators*. Ypsilanti, Mich.: High Scope Press, 1979.

Lindberg, L., and Swedlow, R. *Early Childhood Education: A Guide for Observation and Participation*. Boston: Allyn and Bacon, 1980.

CHAPTER 9

Adapting the Curriculum for Bilingual Classrooms

Since the advent of federal funding for bilingual education in 1968, school districts serving children whose first language is not English have initiated programs to facilitate optimal learning in bilingual children. Compared to education in the United States generally, bilingual education, with a brief fifteen-year history, is still in the early stages of development. Bilingual educators, whether they are administering federal programs or teaching, are struggling to design and implement curricula for bilingual children that use the child's first language and at the same time introduce and develop the child's ability to use English.

The Bilingual Education Act passed by Congress in 1968 included guidelines and funding to provide instruction in their native language for non–English-speaking students. In 1975 the U.S. Commission on Civil Rights further stressed that instructors of bilingual children must be able to communicate in the child's language (U.S. Commission on Civil Rights, 1975). Since funding was initiated, bilingual projects have been conducted for more than sixty language groups; however, Ornstein and Levine (1982) report that 70 percent of the children in the projects are Hispanic.

The Supreme Court ruling in *Lau vs. Nichols* in 1974 has also had an effect on the expansion of bilingual education. As a result of *Lau vs. Nichols*, the Office of Civil Rights enforced policies requiring school districts to improve educational programs for limited-English speakers as well as non-English speakers in the schools.

Prior to the bilingual legislation in 1968, most children were taught using the immersion method. That is, the English language was taught exclusively, and all students were taught as if they were native English speakers (Garcia, 1982). Since the advent of bilingual education, two approaches have been used for bilingual programs, the transitional model and the maintenance model. In *transitional* or ESL (English as a Second Language) programs the purpose is to develop the child's facility in English. Instruction in the native language is used as a bridge to instruction in English. Garcia described transition programs as having the following characteristics:

1. A specific concern is shown for the teaching of English language in a formal sense.
2. A remedial/compensatory (catch up) perspective is exemplified.
3. Native language-speaking aides are extensively used in lieu of bilingual teaching staff.
4. Native language instruction in a formal sense is nonexistent.
5. The overall curriculum does not integrate aspects of the ESL Program. ESL instruction is taught as a separate curricular unit (1982, p. 96).

In the *maintenance* approach to bilingual education, children are taught in two languages. The objectives of the maintenance can range from continued development of both languages to eventual total immersion in English. To maintain both languages, teachers first instruct the children in the home language and introduce English as a second language. As the children increase in their ability to use English, more instruction is presented in English, but the home language is also maintained and developed so that the child will eventually be able to use both languages equally well. Garcia characterized maintenance programs as follows:

1. Team teaching is employed either by pairing monolingual English and bilingual professional staff or though staffing the classroom with single bilingual professional classroom staffing.
2. The native language is used extensively in subject content areas.
3. Instruction of language (both aspects of the native language and English) is most likely integrated into various subject content areas.
4. An extensive effort is made to incorporate relevant cultural learning activities in the curriculum. These activities usually take on a multicultural characteristic.
5. Monolingual English-speaking children are included in the class and are given instruction in the non-English-speaking children's language.
6. Monolingual English-speaking children that are of the same ethnic group as the non-English-speaking children are encouraged to participate in an attempt to restore their native language (Ibid.).

Although it is too soon to know which model of bilingual education will eventually be advocated for standard use in the schools, both seem to be equally popular at this time. There are controversies surrounding both approaches. Proponents of the maintenance approach stress it will build a strong self-concept or sense of identity in the children, while opponents express concern that it will discourage children from learning English. Another controversy is related to the staffing of bilingual programs. Those who favor transitional programs assert that the latter need fewer bilingual instructors than do maintenance programs (Ornstein and Levine, 1982).

Research on the effectiveness of the two approaches is tentative and inconclusive. Because there are few sound evaluations available that can compare transitional versus maintenance programs, any conclusions on the relative effectiveness of the strategies must await additional research.

MEETING THE NEEDS OF BILINGUAL CHILDREN IN EARLY CHILDHOOD

Young children who come from homes where languages other than English are spoken enter day care, nursery schools, kindergarten, and public school programs with varying abilities in two languages. These variations range from knowing only the home language, on the one hand, to being highly verbal in English but with a large receptive vocabulary in the home language, on the other. Some children are balanced bilinguals; they have an equal facility in both languages. Other children are stronger in one language, but do not seem to have a large vocabulary in either language. Consequently, teachers must be concerned with not only what kind of bilingual instruction to use but also how to adapt the curriculum to all the types of bilinguality represented in their classrooms.

Bilingual children not only come from homes where different languages are spoken, but they represent cultures that are different from Anglo middle-class culture. Studies of language and cultural differences have yielded information that affects our ideas of how culturally and linguistically different children should be instructed.

Ramirez and Castaneda (1974) studied learning styles of Hispanic children, which they labeled *bicognitive*. They found Hispanic children to be more "field sensitive" than nonminority students. Because they are more influenced by personal relationships and by praise or disapproval, instruction for Hispanic children shoud include humor, drama, and fantasy. Ramirez and Castaneda proposed that instruction should be structured so that children are able to work cooperatively with other students and the teacher. Kagan and Madsen (1971) also found behavioral style differences when comparing cultures. They reported that Mexican and Mexican-American children perform best on tasks that require cooperation, while European-American children perform best on tasks that require competition.

Competition is also frowned on in the Navajo culture. When reservation children would not volunteer to answer questions because it would indicate rudeness to peers, Cooper (1979) reported that the teacher solved the problem by changing teaching methods. When Navajo students were no longer required to compete, their learning was improved.

John-Steiner and Smith (1978) found that classroom instruction for Pueblo children needs to be more compatible with how the children learn outside the school. John-Steiner and Smith determined that Pueblo children learn through involvement with a significant person in their lives. They also benefit from verbal instruction and exploratory play.

Instructors of bilingual children use many different strategies and instruments to determine the bilingual child's language and learning needs and abilities. To assess language levels, schools often use standardized language assessment tests such as the Bilingual Syntax Measure or the Language Assessment Battery. Through instruments such as these, which are administered orally on a one-to-one basis in both languages, the teacher tries to determine how well the child functions in each language. The difficulty with using any of the standardized language tests is that they are imprecise and lack reliability in measuring how the child understands and speaks the two languages. Another difficulty in using standardized instruments arises because how the child thinks in terms of the two languages cannot be measured by the instruments presently available for teachers to use.

There are informal methods that teachers also utilize to determine language facility. One is to record the child speaking both languages and then analyze the recording to evaluate vocabulary, syntax, and other language indicators in both languages. Listening to the child in natural play situations can also reveal which language is used most comfortably, or whether both are used with confidence. Whatever methods are employed to determine language ability, the teacher should be constantly alert to incidental clues of language usage and modify instruction when indicated in order to serve the child's language needs better.

If teachers could group children by language facility alone, they would consider the task complex enough. In reality, the individual bilingual child also enters school possessing a unique background of learning and cultural experiences, ability and maturity. Just as the English-speaking child is assessed and grouped according to the learning level already achieved, so the bilingual child must also be evaluated in terms of cognitive learning and other types of development brought to school. In order to form learning groups that will meet both the cognitive and the language needs of each child, the teacher must combine the children's learning accomplishments and needs with the determination of language development in each language.

Children of different cultural groups may have different cognitive styles. Hilliard and Vaughn-Scott (1982) reported that "some individuals and groups prefer to deal analytically with the world, comprehending it by breaking it down into small parts. Others prefer to deal with the world and with experiences in general by approaches that are more holistic . . ." (p. 183).

The effect that bilingualism has on cognition has been studied, but any cause-and-effect relationship must be considered carefully. Cultural experiences affect cognition. Ramirez and Castaneda (1974) found a strong relationship between cultural experiences and cognitive style. Although any conclusions made relating bilingualism and cognition are tentative, Garcia proposed the following:

1. bilingual children have been found to score both higher and lower than monolingual children on specific and general measures of cognitive development, intelligence, and school environment;
2. balanced bilingual children have outperformed monolingual children and unbalanced bilingual children on specific cognitive tasks (1982, p. 95).

DESIGNING INSTRUCTION FOR BILINGUAL CHILDREN

Whatever philosophy of bilingual education is implemented in an early childhood program, some of the methods to be used with teaching concepts are compatible with either the maintenance or the transitional model.

When introducing new concepts to children who are first-language speakers or who function more comfortably in the home language, the teacher always introduces the new concept in the home language. The sequence of designing activities to begin with the concrete and move to the abstract remains consistent; however, the initial instruction is conducted in the home language. When the teacher feels that the child understands the concept and has acquired in the home language any vocabulary connected with the concept, then instruction in English can begin.

When introducing the English instruction with the concept, the teacher does not reteach the concept but rather works with it as a language lesson. The child already has a grasp of the concept in the home language. Now the child learns the English language used with the concept. This process of teaching the concept first in the home language followed by teaching the English language to go with the concept is used by both the maintenance and transitional models of bilingual instruction. In the transitional model this strategy would be gradually eliminated when the child has acquired enough English to manage all instruction in English, whereas in the maintenance model the strategy would be maintained.

USING THE DEVELOPMENTAL CHECKLIST FOR BILINGUAL INSTRUCTION

To facilitate the use of the Frost Wortham Developmental Checklist with bilingual children whose first language is Spanish, a Spanish translation has been developed. The Spanish translation is identical to the English version. Checklists for other languages can also be developed from the English version.

For children learning concepts in Spanish, teachers may use the Spanish version for grouping and recordkeeping purposes. Mastery of the concept can be recorded on the Spanish checklist. The English checklist can then be used to record the acquisition of the English vocabulary and language for the concept. Later, if all instruction is transferred to English, the English checklist can be used as the recordkeeping instrument for mastery of the concept introduced and mastered in English. In a maintenance model, both language versions of the checklist can be used throughout the school experience.

The reading readiness checklist will be used in a slightly different manner with bilingual children. Although most of the skills that indicate readiness are the same for both languages, the alphabet is different. As a result, objectives related to letter sounds, letter names, and alphabetical order must be taught separately for both languages.

Teachers often believe that all reading readiness skills must be taught in both languages. This is a mistaken idea. Once the child has developed such readiness skills as auditory discrimination, visual discrimination, and directionality in one language, the mastery of the skill is generated to the second language.

SPANISH TRANSLATION OF DEVELOPMENTAL CHECKLIST— DESAROLLOS PREESCOLAR (PRESCHOOL DEVELOPMENT)

DESARROLLO DE LENGUAJE PREESCOLAR
Lenguaje Oral (café)*

NIVEL III			
1. La mayor parte del lenguaje es inteligible			
2. Reconoce y nombra objetos comunes			
3. Responde correctamente a instrucciones simples referentes a situaciones dentro de la sala de clase			
4. Usa oraciones de cuatro a cinco palabras			
5. Hace preguntas para adquirir información sobre cómo resolver problemas			
NIVEL IV			
1. Usa palabras simples que indican posición (*encima, debajo*)			
2. Usa palabras simples de acción (*correr, andar*)			

SPANISH TRANSLATION OF DEVELOPMENTAL CHECKLIST (continued)

3. Usa oraciones completas			
4. Usa lenguaje para determinaciones específicas (direcciones, información)			
5. Verbaliza eventos rutinales ("vamos a jugar afuera")			
6. Usa un promedio de cinco palabras por oración			
7. Sigue instrucciones simples			
8. Repite cuentos de niños			

NIVEL V

1. Comunica ideas, sentimientos y emociones en oraciones bien formuladas			
2. Usa la forma correcta de la mayoría de los verbos en conversación informal			
3. Usa preposiciones correctas para indicar sitio y posición			
4. Usa casi todos los pronombres personales correctamente			
5. Explica el mecanismo de aparatos simples (sacapuntas, por ejemplo)			
6. Usa lenguaje para obtener lo que desea			
7. Puede seguir instrucciones que contengan tres partes			

*Developed by Joe Frost and Sue Wortham; revised September 1976. Translated by Enriqueta G. Olivares (April 1978). Used by permission of Joe L. Frost.

Preparación Literaria (amarillo)*

NIVEL V

Discriminación auditiva y visual			
1. Discrimina entre sonidos semejantes formados por diferentes objetos			
2. Discrimina entre fonéticos iniciales (*bat/cat, fat/rat, plat/flat, sat/hat, fan/Dan*)			
3. Discrimina entre fonéticos centrales (*bet/bit, bat/ban, bit/bat, bin/ban, bot/bat*)			
4. Discrimina entre fonéticos finales (*bat/ban, can/cad, bet/bed*)			

**SPANISH TRANSLATION OF DEVELOPMENTAL
CHECKLIST (continued)**

5. Sigue con sus ojos objetos movibles de lado a lado a distancia de poderlos leer			
6. Dibuja círculos con ambos cabos unidos			
7. Copia letras del alfabeto y figuras de ejemplares			
8. Con lápiz traza lineas rectas para conectar puntos			
9. Copia dibujos de objetos arreglados en orden			
10. Dibuja objetos antes de que son arreglados en orden			
11. Discrimina entre semejanzas y diferencias de dibujos pintados			
12. Escoge palabras iguales y símbolos de alguna página impresa.			
13. Identifica su nombre impreso			
14. Aparéa letras mayúsculas y minúsculas			
15. Identifica las letras del alfabeto			
16. Identifica palabras que aparecen en escritos conocidos			
17. Cuenta de experiencias acerca de una historia ya conocida			
18. Sugiere títulos para historias que haya experimentado			
19. Repite experiencias en forma organizada			
20. Sigue el índice de izquierda a derecha con progresión al estarle leyendo un adulto			
Destrezas de comprensión			
1. Escucha y sigue direcciones verbales			
2. Coloca elementos en un dibujo (más alto, más largo)			
3. Repite un cuento en el orden de sucesión que se le haya leído			
4. Contesta preguntas que recuerda acerca del cuento			
5. Se forma analogías del cuento sobre sus propias experiencias			
6. Pronóstica y/o construye la conclusión de cuentos			
7. Reorganiza dibujos para mostrar la sucesión correcta del cuento.			
8. Hace decisiones importantes acerca de los eventos del cuento			

*Developed by Joe Frost and Sue Wortham; revised September 1976. Translated by Enriqueta G. Olivares (April 1978). Used by permission of Joe L. Frost.

DESARROLLO MÓVIL PREESCOLAR
**Coordinación (azul)* (Movible, delicada y corpulente;
mano-ojo; destrezas por su propio esfuerzo)
Movimiento Corpulento**

NIVEL III			
1. Pesca la pelota con sus dos manos sobre su pecho			
2. Camina sobre un balancín de seis pies			
3. Salta con los dos pies varias veces, sin ayuda			
4. Tira la pelota a cinco pies con diligencia			
5. Sube y baja el resbaladero			
6. Sube alternando sus pies cogiéndose del pasamanos			
7. Se para sobre un pie y se balancéa brevemente			
8. Empuja una carretilla cargada			
9. Corre libremente sin tropezarse ni caerse			
10. Construye torres con nueve o diez bloques			
NIVEL IV			
1. Se balancéa en un pie			
2. Camina sobre raya recta para adelante y para atrás			
3. Sube escalones con sus pies alternativamente, sin ayuda			
4. Se sube al "Gimnasia Selva"			
5. Brinca desconfiadamente			
6. Pasea en triciclo			
7. Tira, pesca y rebota pelota grande			
8. Acomoda bloques verticalemente y horizontalmente			
9. Forma estructuras reconocidas con bloques			
10. Pasea en triciclo fácilmente con velocidad y destreza			
NIVEL V			
1. Pesca y tria pelota chica			
2. Rebota y pesca pelota chica			
3. Brinca con cualquier pie			
4. Brinca la cuerda			
5. Salta en un pie			
6. Arma juguetes de latón y forma estructuras con bloques			
7. Martilla y serrucha con cierta destreza			

SPANISH TRANSLATION OF DEVELOPMENTAL CHECKLIST (continued)

8.	Camina sobre un balancín para adelante y para atrás		
9.	Baja escalones alternando sus pies		

*Developed by Joe Frost and Sue Wortham; revised September 1976. Translated by Enriqueta G. Olivares (April 1978). Used by permission of Joe L. Frost.

Movimiento Delicado*

NIVEL III			
1. Coloca clavijas pequeñas en un tablero			
2. Coge el pincel o lápiz con toda la mano			
3. Come con cuchara			
4. Se abrocha botones grandes en su propia ropa			
5. Sólito se pone su saco			
6. Ensarta cuentas con facilidad			
7. Con exactitud martilla un juguete machacado			
8. Arma un rompecabezas de tres o cuatro pedazos			
NIVEL IV			
1. Bate y enrolla barro			
2. Arma un rompecabezas de cinco pedazos			
3. Forma un diseño de clavijas			
4. Corta con tijera y pega descuidadamente			
5. Come correctamente con tenedor			
6. Sostiene la taza con una mano			
7. Cuelga su saco en le colgador o en el gancho			
8. Manipula creyones o pinceles grandes			
9. Abrocha botones y cierra cierres automáticos con facilidad			
NIVEL V			
1. Corta y pega diseños creativos			
2. Forma diferentes diseños con clavijas			
3. Abrocha botones, cierra cierres automáticos y amarra cordones de zapatos			

SPANISH TRANSLATION OF DEVELOPMENTAL CHECKLIST (continued)

4. Hace objetos reconocidos de barro			
5. Se atiende a sí mismo en el baño			
6. Come independientemente			
7. Se viste y se desviste independientemente			
8. Coge y manipula lápices, creyones y pinceles de varios tamaños			
9. Se peina y se cepilla			
10. Come con cuchillo y tenedor			
11. Se abrocha los zapatos			
12. Arma rompecabezas de doce pedazos			

*Developed by Joe Frost and Sue Wortham; revised September 1976. Translated by Enriqueta G. Olivares (April 1978). Used by permission of Joe L. Frost.

DESARROLLO SOCIAL PREESCOLAR
Juego Social Y Socializándose (verde)*
(Entre y dentro relaciones personales y juego)

NIVEL III			
1. Se ajusta a juego independiente			
2. Se ajusta a juego paralelo			
3. Juega brevemente con sus compañeros			
4. Reconoce las necesidades de otros			
5. Demuestra simpatía por otros			
6. Participa en actividades por diez o quince minutos			
7. Canta canciones simples			
NIVEL IV			
1. Se desprende de su mamá de buena gana			
2. Platica con otros niños			
3. Platica con adultos			
4. Juega con sus compañeros			
5. Coopera en las rutinas de la sala de clase			
6. Acepta turnos y comparte			
7. Reemplaza materiales después de usarlos			

SPANISH TRANSLATION OF DEVELOPMENTAL CHECKLIST (continued)

8. Cuida de sus posesiones personales			
9. Respeta lo ajeno			
10. Participa en alguna actividad por quince o veinte minutos			
11. Participa en actividades en grupos de banda musical			
12. Canta con el grupo			
13. Es sensitivo a alargar y criticar			

NIVEL V

1. Termina casi todos los proyectos iniciados por sí mismo			
2. Trabaja y juega bajo limitada supervisión			
3. Participa en juego cooperativo			
4. Escucha mientras sus compañeros hablan			
5. Sigue direcciones múltiples y de dilación			
6. Lleva adelante responsabilidades especiales (da de comer al animal, etcétera)			
7. Escucha y sigue sugestiones de adultos			
8. Hace mandatos simples			
9. Goza platicar con adultos			
10. Tolera espacio de tiempo para una variedad de obligaciones			
11. Evalúa su trabajo; sugiere mejoramientos			

*Developed by Joe Frost and Sue Wortham; revised September 1976. Translated by Enriqueta G. Olivares (April 1978). Used by permission of Joe L. Frost.

Representación Dramática (morado)*
(Simbolizando y limitando)

NIVEL III

1. Imita a personas mayores (juega a la casa, a la tienda)			
2. Expresa contratiempos en el juego			
3. Produce imaginariamente compañeros de juego			
4. Participa en asuntos domésticos			
5. Pinta y dibuja figuras simbólicas en papel grande			

SPANISH TRANSLATION OF DEVELOPMENTAL CHECKLIST (continued)

6. Construye estructuras simples, con bloques			
7. Usa juguetes de transportación, gente y animales para enriquecer el juego de bloques			
8. Se imagina que cualquier objeto es el objeto que él desea (facultad simbólica)			
NIVEL IV			
1. El funcionamiento representa una variedad extensa de funciones en el centro doméstico y otros centros			
2. La función representa una variedad extensa de ocupaciones de adultos			
3. Toma parte en dramatizaciones de cuentos conocidos			
4. Usa títeres en diálogos iniciados por sí mismo			
5. Comprende la diferencía entre lo real y lo fingido			
6. Pretende que las muñecas son verdadera gente			
7. Canta solo			
8. Construye (pinta, moldea, etcétera) figuras reconocidas			
9. Participa en juegos meniques			
NIVEL V			
1. Toma parte en el funcionamiento de un centro doméstico			
2. Funciona en el patio de recreo			
3. Funciona en ocupaciones de adulto			
4. Reconoce que las pinturas representan verdaderos objetos			
5. Participa en una variedad extensa de actividades creativas: juegos meniques, banda rítmica, trabajos con barro, pinturas, juegos en el patio de recreo, trabajos domésticos, canto, etcétera			
6. Produce objetos en la mesa de carpintería; habla de ellos			
7. Produce objetos de arte; habla de ellos			
8. Busca mejores maneras para construir			
9. Construye estructuras complicadas de bloques			

*Developed by Joe Frost and Sue Wortham; revised September 1976. Translated by Enriqueta G. Olivares (April 1978). Used by permission of Joe L. Frost.

DESARROLLO DE CONCEPTOS PREESCOLAR
Destrezas en Identificación y Clasificación (rojo)*

NIVEL III			
1. Discrimina entre dos olores			
2. Sabe y verbaliza que los olores son "diferentes"	·		
3. Puede señalar verbalmente olor u olores			
4. Discrimina entre dos sonidos y verbaliza que son "diferentes."			
5. Puede señalar sabor o sabores verbalmente.			
6. Puede señalar sonidos verbalmente			
7. Apunta a diferentes objetos de comida si se le pide			
8. Apunta a formas básicas si se le pide (círculo, cuadrado, triángulo)			
9. Identifica conceptos de tiempo en general (temprano, tarde, hoy, mañana)			
NIVEL IV			
1. Identifica formas básicas (círculo, cuadrado, triángulo, rectángulo)			
2. Discrimina diferencia de tamaño y forma de objetos (grande, chico, largo, corto, cuadrado, redondo)			
3. Clasifica objetos por peso (pesado, liviano)			
4. Clasifica objetos por altura (alto, corto)			
5. Identifica los colores fundamentales (rojo, amarillo, azul)			
6. Discrimina semejanzas y diferencias (tamaño, forma, color, etcétera)			
7. Discrimina diferencias opuestas en:			
a) sonido (fuerte/suave)			
b) distancia (lejos/cerca)			
c) peso (pesado/liviano)			
d) tiempo (largo/corto)			
NIVEL V			
1. Identifica y señala relaciones espaciales:			
a) lejos/cerca			
b) dentro/fuera			
c) delante/atrás			

SPANISH TRANSLATION OF DEVELOPMENTAL CHECKLIST (continued)

d) arriba/abajo			
e) encima/debajo, etcétera			
2. Identifica y discrimina relaciones de valores:			
a) bien/mal			
b) bueno/malo			
c) bonito/feo			
d) triste/alegre			
e) gusto/disgusto			
3. Identifica y discrimina relaciones pertenecientes al tiempo:			
a) día/noche			
b) hoy/mañana			
c) ayer/hoy			
d) antes/después			
e) ahora/luego			
f) más temprano/más tarde			
4. Identifica y discrimina acciones:			
a) correr			
b) andar			
c) brincar, etcétera			
5. Identifica y discrimina opuestos:			
a) duro/blando			
b) alto/bajo			
c) lleno/vacío			
6. Identifica colores secundarios (verde y naranjado, por ejemplo)			
7. Identifica las propiedades simples de un objeto (color, forma, tamaño)			
8. Clasifica colores por intensidad (obscuro, claro, más obscuro que, más claro que)			
9. Clasifica alimentos (frutas, vegetales, carne)			
10. Clasifica sabores:			
a) dulce			
b) agrio			
c) salado			
d) amargo			
11. Clasifica superficies por textura:			
a) liso			
b) áspero			
c) blando			

SPANISH TRANSLATION OF DEVELOPMENTAL CHECKLIST (continued)

d) duro			
12. Identifica y clasifica la forma de objetos comunes:			
a) círculo			
b) cuadrado			
c) rectángulo			
d) triángulo			
13. Clasifica objetos por más de una calidad			
14. Pone objetos en orden por tamaño			
15. Arregla sonidos por volumen			
16. Explica el funcionamiento de objetos simples			
17. Invierte operaciones simples:			
a) amontona/desmontona			
b) arregla/desarregla/vuelve a arreglar			
18. Clasifica por medio de condición:			
a) caliente/frío			
b) mojado/seco			
c) viejo/nuevo, etcétera			
19. Clasifica por medio de función:			
a) alimento/comer			
b) vehículo/paseo			

*Developed by Joe Frost and Sue Wortham; revised September 1976. Translated by Enriqueta G. Olivares (April 1978). Used by permission of Joe L. Frost.

Cuantitativo y Solución de Problemas (naranjado)*

NIVEL III			
1. Manipula y experimenta con maquinaria simple			
2. Cuenta de memoria del uno hasta el cinco			
3. Tiene concepto de números ordinales hasta el tercero			
4. Identifica moneda:			
a) un centavo			
b) cinco centavos			
c) diez centavos			
5. Desarrolla el concepto de valor de dinero			
6. Forma diseños creativos con materiales			
7. Usa materiales (relativos) para proyectos múltiples			

SPANISH TRANSLATION OF DEVELOPMENTAL CHECKLIST (continued)

NIVEL IV			
1. Identifica pares de objetos conocidos:			
a) zapatos			
b) calcetines			
c) guantes			
d) aretes, etcétera			
2. Usa conceptos ordinales hasta el quinto			
3. Demuestra el concepto de números hasta el diez			
4. Identifica:			
a) un centavo			
b) cinco centavos			
c) diez centavos			
d) una peseta			
e) un dólar			
5. Compara distancia (altura, anchura) con un objeto independiente (un palo, etcétera)			
6. Compara diferencia en dimensión (más alto, más bajo, más delgado, etcétera)			
7. Compara volumen en recipientes separados. Describe objetos de diferentes perspectivas visuales			
NIVEL V			
1. Compara métodos para llenar un espacio			
2. Agrupa objetos en juegos de igual número			
3. Compara elementos de juegos no iguales (más que, menos qué, etcétera)			
4. Puede mostrar lo que corresponde "uno-a-uno" (one-to-one correspondence). Ejemplar: cinco manzanas para cinco niños			
5. Cuenta hasta el cien			
6. Demuestra el concepto de números hasta el veinticinco			
7. Ordena números del uno al diez			
8. Identifica números en grupo (marca cinco carros)			
9. Combina (suma el número total en dos grupos chicos)			
10. Usa conceptos ordinales hasta el décimo			

*Developed by Joe Frost and Sue Wortham; revised September 1976. Translated by Enriqueta G. Olivares (April 1978). Used by permission of Joe L. Frost.

SUMMARY

Many children attending early childhood programs come from homes where languages other than English are spoken. Children who come to school with various facilities in two languages have special learning needs. Bilingual programs implemented since funding was passed by Congress in 1968 use special teaching strategies to meet the educational needs of bilingual children.

Experts do not agree on what type of bilingual education provides the best curriculum for helping bilingual and bicultural children succeed in school. The transitional or English-as-a-Second-Language approach focuses on teaching the child to speak English and learn from English instruction as soon as possible. Instruction in the child's native language is used only as long as students need it before they are able to function in English. The maintenance approach to bilingual education values the child's home language. The child receives instruction in both languages. Even after the child achieves facility in English, teachers also maintain and develop the home language as a vehicle for instruction.

Bilingual children come from various cultures. Their cultural background is frequently at odds with the cultural values prevalent in the schools. Whereas American culture has traditionally stressed competition, some cultures value cooperation instead. Educators in bilingual and bicultural programs need to be sensitive to differences in behavioral and learning styles present in children from various cultural backgrounds.

Teachers of bilingual children face many challenges in designing appropriate instruction for bilingual children. The immediate task is to determine the child's facility in English and the home language. In implementing learning experiences, the teacher has to work with language development and cognitive development simultaneously. Because research to date has provided no definitive answers as to the best instructional method to use with bilingual children, teachers will continue to innovate and evaluate as they teach the bilingual children in their care.

REFERENCES

Cooper, G. "Issues in Cross-Cultural Communications." *New Directions* (April 1979): 18–19.

Garcia, E. "Bilingualism in Early Childhood." In J. F. Brown (ed.). *Curriculum Planning for Young Children*. Washington, D.C.: National Association for the Education of Young Children, 1982.

Hilliard, A. G., and Vaughn-Scott, M. "The Quest for the 'Minority' Child." In S. G. Moore and C. R. Cooper (eds.). *The Young Child Reviews of Research, Volume 3*. Washington, D.C.: National Association for the Education of Young Children, 1982.

John-Steiner. V., and Smith, L. "The Educational Promise of Cultural Pluralism."

Paper presented for National Conference on Urban Education, St. Louis, Missouri, 1978.

Kagan, S., and Madsen, M. C. "Cooperation and Competition of Mexican and Anglo-American Children of Two Years Under Instructional Sets." *Developmental Psychology* 5, no. 5 (1971): 32–39.

Ornstein, A. C., and Levine, D. U. "Multicultural Education: Trends and Issues." *Childhood Education* 58, no. 4 (1982): 241–245.

Ramirez, M. and Castaneda, A. *Cultural Democracy, Bicognitive Development and Education*. New York: Academic Press, 1974.

U.S. Commission on Civil Rights. *Toward Quality Education for Mexican Americans. Report IV: Mexican American Education Study*. Washington, D.C.: U.S. Commission on Civil Rights, 1975.

CHAPTER 10

Adapting the Curriculum for Children with Special Needs

Although an "average" child does not exist, and every child is unique in some way, there are children who function outside the range of normal learning behaviors. At the low end of the spectrum are children who because of some handicapping condition need special attention to learn at their highest potential. At the other end are the gifted children who demonstrate high levels of learning potential. In the past, children with handicapping conditions were taught in separate classrooms, while gifted children were taught in regular classrooms but often received no instruction to facilitate development of their special needs for learning. At the present time more provisions are being made for these children with special needs, but the services are provided as much as possible without totally segregating them from other students of the same age.

MEETING THE NEEDS OF GIFTED CHILDREN

For many years there was little funding to provide the instructional services needed by gifted children. Children who were academically advanced were allowed to be "double-promoted," that is, to skip a grade in school. Individual teachers would often take a special interest in an exceptionally bright student. Nevertheless, the high number of gifted students, especially minority students, who dropped out before completing high school led many educators to campaign for a better education for the gifted. Although funding is now available, the amount is minuscule compared to the enormous amounts of money funded to serve children who achieve below the average range in school. While some schools have pilot programs for the gifted, most districts have the resources to provide only an hour or two of supplementary instruction each week for gifted children. Although these services are a good beginning, gifted children still need more opportunities if they are to become the inventors, national leaders, and creators so badly needed in our world. The major responsibility for reaching gifted children still rests with the classroom teachers.

In the early childhood classroom, some gifted children are easy to identify. Many of them abound with energy and verbal ability. They are eager to discuss and try out ideas. Often the gifted children are early readers, but not necessarily. Some appear to be very bored with regular kindergarten activities. Sometimes gifted children are difficult to manage because they do not readily fit into classroom routines and are adamant in pursuing their own endeavors. In primary classrooms the "dreamers" who appear to lack discipline or good work habits are often gifted children who withdraw into their own world.

DESIGNING CURRICULUM FOR GIFTED CHILDREN

The Frost Wortham Developmental Checklist can be used to identify and serve gifted children. In assessing the young child informally, the teacher may discover that the three-year-old child is working ahead of his or her peers and has mastered most objectives at Levels III and IV on the checklist. Although the chronological age may be three, the child's developmental age is closer to that of the average five year old.

In using the Developmental Checklist, the teacher can readily find experiences at Level V that are appropriate for the gifted three or four year old. Because the activities used on all levels of the checklist are developmentally appropriate for early childhood, activities at any level can be used in the early childhood classroom.

The gifted five year old presents a different problem. Again, the checklist can be used for assessment. If the child has mastered all objectives at Level V, learning experiences may be needed at the first-grade or higher grade level. The teacher may be tempted to secure readers and workbooks from primary-grade teachers to allow the child to progress at a higher academic level; however, the teacher needs to remember that the gifted child in kindergarten resides in a five-year-old body. Instructional materials used for older children may prove to be frustrating for the child. Although the student may be able to function mentally at a second- or third-grade level, his or her physical development may make writing tasks difficult or impossible. The teacher will want to provide reading and other academic experiences that are within the child's ranges of interest and total development. The gifted early childhood student also needs to explore the environment and work at tasks that do not preclude frequent physical activity. For example, the gifted student may need to demonstrate the ability to master math concepts using concrete materials rather than worksheets. The challenge for the teacher is to know the sequence of objectives taught at the primary level but to incorporate knowledge of physical and social development of younger children when designing learning activities for accelerated cognitive learning.

HANDICAPPED CHILDREN

Handicapped children present different challenges for families and schools. Although handicapping conditions can be categorized, each handicapped child is an individual whose unique needs and potential must be accepted and understood. Handicapping conditions include speech impairment, learning disabilities, mental retardation, emotional disturbances, hearing impaired and deafness, visual impairments, and crippling handicaps (National Advisory Committee on the Handicapped, 1976). The list is ordered from most to least common in occurrence.

Speech Impairment

Many young children make errors in speech; however, not all defects indicate a speech handicap. Because young children are in the process of developing speech and language, they frequently make articulation errors that later improve as the child develops. Other errors are not developmental but have a medical basis. Some definite types of speech impairment are poor voice quality, stuttering, cleft palate, distortions in pronunciation, and omissions of sounds from speech. Frequently children have speech problems that are the result of poor hearing.

Learning Disabilities

Learning-disabled children demonstrate difficulties in benefiting from classroom instruction. The difficulty encountered is not the result of a physical impairment but is commonly neurological in origin. Excessive activity or hyperactivity is one type of learning disability. Hyperactive children usually show symptoms before age five and are more often male than female (Lord, 1982). Preschool hyperactive children have been characterized as difficult to manage at home, with unpredictable moods and irregular eating and sleepng habits. They are easily frustrated and are accident prone (Ross and Ross, 1976). A common mistake in classrooms is to label many children hyperactive when they are normal children who are very active and energetic.

Learning-disabled children can have a variety of behaviors that indicate a problem. Some children are overly distractible and have difficulty in concentrating, while others are awkward or have difficulty in remembering. Some children have perceptual difficulties when putting a puzzle together or confuse similar words or letters.

Mental Retardation

Children who are mentally retarded exhibit a developmental delay in intellectual functioning. Children who are retarded experience disorders in maturation, learning, and social skills. They are classified into three categories of retardation: educable mentally retarded (EMR), trainable mentally retarded (TMR), and Down's syndrome. Mental retardation can be caused by medical disorders, risk factors during pregnancy and infancy, and environmental factors. Medical disorders include Down's syndrome and disorders of the body's chemical system, such as phenylketonuria (PKU), which causes mental retardation. Risk factors are conditions before, during or after the child's birth that can impair development. Risk factors include prematurity, the mother's poor nutrition, and low birth weight. Environmental factors that can result in retardation are poor family and health care, limited maternal attachment, and lack of opportunities for social, physical, and adaptive stimulation (Meisels and Anastasiow, 1982). Indications of mental retardation include slow academic progress, delayed language skills, infantile habits, inability to comprehend or follow directions, and delayed coordination of motor skills.

Emotional Disturbances

Emotionally disturbed children also exhibit abnormal behaviors. They may misbehave for no apparent reason, seem depressed or unhappy, overreact to minor incidents, or withdraw from relationships. These children may use negative behavior such as acting out, temper tantrums, disobedience, and aggression (Lord, 1982). Fears and extreme shyness are also related to emotional disturbance.

Autism may be classified as a type of emotional disturbance, although autistic children frequently are also mentally retarded and delayed in language development. Autistic children also use stereotypic (repetitive) movements and may injure themselves (Rutter, 1978).

Hearing Impaired and Deafness

About 16 million Americans have impaired hearing, while a half a million are profoundly deaf (Lundsteen and Tarrow, 1981). The infant with a hearing loss may have impaired development in physical, social, intellectual, and language development (Bronfenbrenner, 1979). Hearing loss can be caused by *otitis media* (inner-ear infections), brain damage, accidents, and other factors (Swick and Palefsky, 1982). Some disorders can be improved through surgery or the use of hearing aids.

Because hearing loss may involve physical and social development, the hearing handicap may be difficult to identify. Some specific indications are when the child does not respond when spoken to or stares straight ahead. Other indications are children using an extremely limited vocabulary or holding the head to one side in an attempt to hear better.

Visual Impairments

Visually handicapped children have difficulty learning from visually oriented materials. Visual handicaps range from enough deviation of vision to require correction with glasses to total blindness. Indications of a visual impairment are frequent blinking, favored use of one eye over the other, and squinting. The visually impaired child may hold objects unusually close or far away, show excessive eye movement, or have watery eyes. Sometimes the child has headaches and dizziness.

Crippling Handicaps

Orthopedically handicapped children may have no intellectual disorders. They may experience frustration when their handicaps prevent them from full participation in classroom activities. Some physically handicapped children must wear prosthetic devices, while others are confined to wheelchairs. Physical facilities in school settings must be designed to include handrails, wheelchair ramps, and wide doorways in order to allow physically handicapped children full access in the educational process.

There are other causes of physical handicaps. Cerebral palsy, malnutrition, diabetes, epilepsy, and cardiac and respiratory disorders can cause physical handicaps. These disorders may also affect the intellectual functioning of the child. Teachers of handicapped children need to be concerned with individual appraisal of children with these disabilities because their learning needs vary.

MEETING THE NEEDS OF HANDICAPPED CHILDREN

There is much that can be done to alleviate the problems associated with handicapped children. As a primary resource, the family, especially the parents' positive or negative attitudes toward the child, will have a profound influence on the child's development. With training and assistance parents can acquire parenting skills that will facilitate the child's development (Meisels and Anastasiow, 1982).

Early childhood intervention programs can also have a positive effect on the child's development. Bettye Caldwell (1970) proposed that the earlier intervention is begun, the more positive is the outlook for the child. Warren Umansky (1982) studied the effectiveness of early intervention and reported that all fourteen early intervention programs studied had a positive effect on the children enrolled. These programs can also prevent more serious conditions from developing and can moderate the trauma the family experiences following the birth of a handicapped child.

The Role of Public Schools

Public Law 94–142, passed in 1975, has drastically changed the manner in which handicapped children are to be instructed in school. Prior to the passage of the law, most handicapped students were taught by special education teachers in separate classrooms or schools. PL 94–142 has made basic changes in services for handicapped learners. Parents are now given a major role in the decisions made for their child's education, and many students are now mainstreamed back into the regular classroom to fulfill the requirements that the child be taught in the least restrictive environment possible (Geren, 1979).

PL 94–142 provides for free and appropriate education for handicapped individuals from ages three to twenty-one. It includes financial assistance to state and local agencies for the education of the handicapped. The law also requires that children be educated in the least restrictive environment, that is, mainstreamed whenever possible into regular classrooms rather than into special classes.

New procedures for identification and educational planning for handicapped children are also a part of PL 94–142. A committee of teachers and administrators, and in some cases diagnosticians, are involved in referral and screening when a child is being considered for special services. More importantly, an individual education plan, or IEP, is required for each handicapped student. The IEP is designed in a meeting that includes the special and regular teachers who will serve the child, an administrator of the school district, the parents, and the child when appropriate. Using assessment information on the child's level of performance as the basis for planning, the IEP is written to include annual goals and short-term objectives for the student's education. Annual goals are reviewed once a year, while objectives may be monitored each week. During the IEP meeting the child's goals and objectives are determined and special and regular teachers describe the strategies and resources that will be used so the student may attain the desired learning (Lowenthal, 1979).

Although Louise Ames (1982) expressed doubts about mainstreaming, successful reports of mainstreaming in developmental programs have been reported by Samuel Meisels (1978), Joan Christopherson (1972), and Robert Bogdan (1983). An important factor is the attitude of teachers and children toward handicapped children. If the child is fully accepted, he or she will feel worthy and competent. When a positive approach is used in working with the handicapped child, a positive outcome is more likely.

Educators and parents often focus on the things the handicapped child cannot do or cannot learn. Phillip Wishon (1982) and Hohmann, Banet, and

Weikart (1979) propose that we should instead concentrate on the child's strengths, or what the child *can* do or learn. Using a developmental approach, teachers should identify the child's status on a developmental continuum and provide developmentally appropriate experiences that will permit the child to exercise emerging abilities. The child is not compared with other children on a chronological basis but is evaluated on a developmental basis, regardless of age.

Teachers who are mainstreaming children into their classrooms have a particular responsibility in meeting the needs of handicapped children within a developmental framework. Mildred Dickerson and Michael Davis (1981) in a developmental approach to mainstreaming believe the role of the teacher is to:

1.   provide quality educational opportunities that are appropriate in content and adapted to the child's mode of learning.
2.   be aware of the processes involved as young children encounter conflicts between their own needs and wishes and their socialization into group living.
3.   be sensitive to the way each child approaches these growth tasks and
4.   be willing to try to meet each child's special needs (p. 9).

Dickerson and Davis also stress that in order to meet each child's special needs, teachers must have a thorough knowledge of normal development. The Frost Wortham Developmental Checklist, with objectives related to all facets of normal development, can serve as a guideline for helping children who are developing in a different way.

USING THE DEVELOPMENTAL CHECKLIST TO WRITE AND IMPLEMENT THE IEP

The Developmenal Checklist is also an excellent tool teachers can use when designing and implementing the IEP within a developmental approach with the handicapped student. Because objectives are sequenced in order of difficulty by level, the teacher has a source for short- and long-range planning for the IEP. Short-term objectives can be taken directly from the checklist and translated into behavioral terms for the IEP.

The Developmental Checklist is especially helpful for teachers of the handicapped because it is arranged by developmental levels rather than by age levels. Handicapped children frequently function at the developmental level of a preschool child even when they are ten years of age or older. Like young children they need learning activities that utilize real experiences and concrete materials.

Teachers of handicapped children report that children who have learning disabilities or handicaps also need a structured, sequential curriculum.

The checklist provides the needed structure and sequence. In addition, it addresses all areas of development, another feature needed by teachers of the handicapped.

As is true for children who learn normally, handicapped children may vary in rate of learning in various levels of development. A child classified as learning disabled with a mild handicapping condition might be developing at a near normal rate in the area of physical development, but progressing very slowly on the checklists related to cognitive development. Children with severe or multiple handicaps may progress very slowly in all areas of development. They are likely to require work on an objective for an extended period of time.

Teachers of handicapped children not only search for learning activities that are developmentally appropriate, they also want objectives to help the children acquire functional skills. Many handicapped children will never learn to read but can acquire the functional skills such as knowing position words and recognizing their name at the prereading level. Many of these skills are prerequisites for training at the prevocational level leading to work in a sheltered workshop.

The activities created for the Developmental Checklist use familiar concrete objects. The use of common objects is suitable for mentally retarded students who need assistance in understanding and organizing their environment. Thus an activity to learn one-to-one correspondence using toothbrushes and toothbrush containers helps students infer relationships that can be transferred to daily living. Children who are blind or deaf could learn from feeling or seeing real objects in order to grasp a concept when pictured objects cannot be used to convey meaning. As a result, activities to identify objects by feeling them in a bag are useful for blind and sighted children equally. Likewise, identification and classification of plastic animal figures results in a verbal response by some children and an equally correct response through signing by deaf students.

Finally, when the Developmental Checklist is used to develop the IEP, it can also be useful as a common framework for communication among the teachers who are serving the handicapped student. Whereas in the past the special education teacher provided all instructional services for handicapped students, responsibility now may be shared with the regular classroom teacher. The Developmental Checklist can assist all teachers who are serving the handicapped student to understand the role each will play in providing instruction. Rather than having each teacher plan for and teach the child separately, combined planning through the development of the IEP results in complementary instruction by each teacher, which enhances the efforts of the others. In addition, classroom teachers have often expected the child who is mainstreamed with age mates to be graded on the basis of regular classroom instruction. The Developmental Checklist, as well as other sequenced skills lists used for IEPs, will help the classroom teacher develop more realistic expectations for the handicapped child in the regular classroom. PL 94–142 essentially requires that instruction be individualized for the needs of each handicapped student. The checklist can help parents and teachers of handicapped children to write and initiate an IEP that is suitable for students who are assessed to be performing at a developmental level similar to that of normal children who are younger chronologically.

SUMMARY

Some children have special learning needs because their development lies outside the normal range in some respect. Gifted children demonstrate high levels of learning potential, while handicapped children suffer from disorders that may impede learning.

Handicapped children may have a speech impairment, a learning disability, mental retardation, an emotional disturbance, a hearing impairment, a visual impairment, an orthopedic impairment, or a combination of handicaps. Although some behaviors exhibited by the child make some handicaps easy to identify, others, such as slight hearing or vision loss, prove to be more difficult.

There is much that can be done to improve the prognosis for the development of handicapped children. Although prevention of handicaps is the ideal, early intervention by parents and intervention programs can minimize the effects of a disorder.

Public Law 94–142, passed in 1975, changed the instructional services provided by public schools for handicapped children. New methods of identifying and planning for instruction were initiated that include parents among the team of professionals that evaluates the child's status and provides an appropriate instructional plan. Most importantly, PL 94–142 required that children be mainstreamed into the regular classroom whenever possible rather than taught in separate, special education classrooms.

Parents and educators who work with handicapped children should take a positive approach to the child's learning by stressing strengths rather than focusing on what the child cannot do. The child should be evaluated according to his or her developmental level rather than by chronological age. Developmentally appropriate experiences will allow the child to progress in a natural manner in keeping with the positive learning potential the child possesses.

The Frost Wortham Developmental Checklist provides a vehicle for educational planning for the young gifted or handicapped child. The checklist can be followed to determine the developmental level of the child in different areas, and individual instructional plans can be designed accordingly. The checklist and activities designed for the checklist will have to be modified for children who have handicaps of physical or sensory origin. Using the other strengths the child possesses, the teacher can adapt activities to enhance the child's modes of learning.

REFERENCES

Ames, L. B. "Mainstreaming: We Have Come Full Circle." *Childhood Education* 58, no. 4 (1982) 238–240.

Bogdan, R. "Does Mainstreaming Work? Is a Silly Question." *Phi Delta Kappan* 64, no. 6 (1983): 427–429.

Bronfenbrenner, U. *The Ecology of Human Development.* Cambridge, Mass.: Harvard University Press, 1979.

Caldwell, B. M. "The Rationale for Early Intervention." *Exceptional Children* 36, no. 10 (1970): 717–726.

Christopherson, J. "The Special Child in the 'Regular' Preschool: Some Administrative Notes." *Childhood Education* 49, 3 (1972): 138–140.

Dickerson, M. G., and Davis, M. D. "The Developmental Approach: A Successful Way to Mainstream the Young Child." *Childhood Education* 58, no. 1 (1981): 8–13.

Geren, K. *Complete Special Education Handbook.* West Nyack, N.Y.: Packer Publishing, 1979.

Hohmann, M.; Banet, B.; and Weikart, D. P. *Young Children in Action.* Ypsilanti, Mich.: High Scope Press, 1979.

Lord, C. "Psychopathology in Early Development." In S. G. Moore and C. R. Cooper (eds.). *The Young Child Review of Research, Volume 3.* Washington, D.C.: National Association for the Education of Young Children, 1982.

Lowenthal, P. "IEP Purposes and Implications." *Young Children* 35 (1979): 28–32.

Lundsteen, S. W., and Tarrow, N. B. *Guiding Young Children's Learning.* New York: McGraw-Hill, 1981.

Meisels, S. J. "Open Education and the Integration of Children with Special Needs." In M. Guralnik (ed.). *Early Intervention and the Integration of Handicapped and Nonhandicapped Childhood.* Baltimore: University Press, 1978.

Meisels, S. J., and Anastasiow, N. J. "The Risks of Prediction: Relationships Between Etiology, Handicapping Conditions, and Developmental Outcomes." In S. G. Moore and C. R. Cooper (eds.). *The Young Child Reviews of Research, Volume 3.* Washington, D.C.: National Association for the Education of Young Children, 1982.

National Advisory Committee on the Handicapped. *The Unfinished Revolution: Education for the Handicapped, 1976 Annual Report.* Washington, D.C.: U.S. Government Printing Office, 1976.

Ross, D. M., and Ross, S. A. *Hyperactivity: Research, Theory, Action.* New York: Wiley, 1976.

Rutter, M. "Diagnosis and Definition." In M. Rutter and E. Schopler (eds.). *Autism: A Reappraisal of Concepts and Treatment.* New York: Plenum, 1978.

State Program Implementation Studies Branch. *Progress Toward a Free Appropriate Public Education: A Report to Congress on the Implementation of PL 94–142.* Washington, D.C.: Bureau of Education for the Handicapped, U.S. Office of Education, 1975.

Swick, K., and Palefsky, E. "Severe Hearing Losses in Infancy: Is Language Development Impaired?" *Childhood Education* 59, 1 (1982): 46–50.

Umansky, W. "More Than a Teacher: An Approach to Meeting Children's Special Needs." *Childhood Education* 58, no. 2 (1982): 155–158.

Wishon, P. M. "Serving Handicapped Young Children: Six Imperatives." *Young Children* 38 (1982): 28–32.

APPENDIX A

Validity and Reliability Data for the Frost Wortham Developmental Checklist

The validity and reliability of the Frost Wortham Developmental Checklist was established by testing checklist objectives with 450 children aged three to five years in day-care centers in San Antonio, Texas. Twenty graduate students working in pairs tested the set of checklists at Levels III, IV, or V with at least fifteen children from at least two different centers. Children in the two centers were representative of different socioeconomic and ethnic groups in the community. That is, if one center had a population of predominantly middle-class children of one ethnic group, the second center chosen had different socioeconomic and ethnic populations. Two pairs of students worked with Level III checklists, three pairs with Level IV checklists, and five pairs with Level V checklists. (Because the Oral Language and Reading Readiness objectives were derived from sources that are commonly known and substantiated by research, the process was not repeated in these two categories.)

Each pair of graduate students worked as a team in administering tasks for checklist items. One member of the pair administered the tasks, while the other recorded responses. Tasks to test the objectives were provided by me or designed by the students. Reliability and validity of checklist items were determined by using the following procedures:

1. Each pair of students met with me to review the tasks and procedures to follow in administering each task. Materials for each task were checked for appropriateness and consistency between teams.
2. Each pair of students established task and interrater reliability by testing each task with children who were not to be part of the sample used

in the study. If lack of clarity in materials or procedures resulted, alterations were made and the process was repeated.

3. Each objective was tested with at least thirty children in at least two different day-care centers representing contrasting socioeconomic groups in the community. The children tested had a range of birth dates within the age level and represented a cross section of ethnic groups. If results for an individual child were unclear, notations were made of the circumstances involved.

4. Testing results were evaluated to determine whether each objective was placed correctly on the checklist. An item was considered correctly placed if at least ten children could, and at least ten children could not, complete the task successfully. For checklist items including several subcomponents, partial mastery was included with full mastery when determining the percentage of students who were successful or unsuccessful on the objective.

Following analysis of the data, seven objectives on the Quantitative and Problem-Solving Checklist and six objectives on the Identification, Discrimination, and Classification Checklist were found to be incorrectly placed. These objectives were moved to a higher or lower level and retested using the same procedures. All but two objectives were found to be correctly placed on the retest. On two other objectives, inconclusive results were reported. To retest these objectives, a different but equivalent task was used. Results on the second task confirmed correct placement of the objectives in question.

Figure 3 shows the form used by teams to administer and record results on individual checklist items.

FIGURE 3

Category _____

Level _____

Objective _____

Investigators _____

_____

Center _____

Names	Age	Ethnic	Result	Comments
1.				
2.				
3.				
4.				
5.				
6.				
7.				
8.				
9.				
10.				
11.				
12.				
13.				
14.				
15.				

APPENDIX **B**

Observation Strategies

To learn about what children are like and how they learn, there is no substitute for teacher observation. Unless teachers plan specifically to observe children, they can lose much valuable insight into the unique nature of each child. Observations may be general, as when the teacher uses anecdotal comments about children, or specific, as when the teacher determines a child's progress or mastery of measurable items on a checklist through observation of specific behaviors.

ANECDOTAL OBSERVATIONS

Teachers spend most of their time in the classroom working with children; however, because teachers are distracted by the responsibilities of classroom management and by their teaching role, they tend to focus on the children as a total group. To expand their understanding of individual children, teachers use observation combined with anecdotal notations to maintain continuing information of student growth. Observations may be made for incidental insight about children or for problem-solving purposes. The following suggestions can facilitate productive observations:

1. Select a time in the schedule when children are naturally engaged in the desired activity or behavior.
2. Be unobtrusive in observation. Try not to have the observation become

distracting to the children. If writing is disturbing to the children, wait and record information when the observation is completed.
3.   Before beginning the observation, mentally review the purpose of the observation and the information desired. Decide what information is to be recorded, such as children's language, or examples of behaviors.
4.   Remember that much information is gained from incidental observations during regular classroom routines. Be prepared to jot down notes that can be expanded later at a more convenient time.

OBSERVATIONS FOR SPECIFIC OBJECTIVES

Often teachers need to determine progress or mastery of specific behaviors or learning objectives. Observation is used to supplement teacher-directed activities for assessment or evaluation. The following suggestions will help the teacher focus on the behaviors to be observed:

1.   Determine the information desired from the observation. If a checklist objective is to be assessed, determine the behaviors that will indicate the child's acquisition or mastery of the objective.
2.   Study the classroom setting to determine if materials and center arrangement are appropriate for the observation. Make any changes necessary prior to observing.
3.   Review what teacher behaviors might be necessary in order to initiate the behaviors to be observed. Will teacher questioning or suggestions be needed to guide a child in the activity to be observed? If so, determine the correct actions the teacher should use.
4.   Determine what recordkeeping materials are needed to record observation results. If a checklist is to be used, have it accessible for recording observations.
5.   If observation information is to be transferred to other forms of records, make all entries as soon as possible so that essential information is not lost or forgotten. Timely recordkeeping also prevents a backlog of records from accumulating.

Index